THE TORONTO MAPLE LEAFS

The Stories & Players behind the Legendary Team

The Publisher: OverTime Books is an imprint of Éditions de la Montagne Verte

Library and Archives Canada Cataloguing in Publication

Poulton, J. Alexander (Jay Alexander), 1977–
   The Toronto Maple Leafs: the stories & players behind the legendary team / J. Alexander Poulton.

ISBN-13: 978-1-897277-16-4
ISBN-10: 1-897277-16-4

1. Toronto Maple Leafs (Hockey team)—History. I. Title.

GV848.T6P69 2007   796.962'6409713541   C2006-906835-6

Project Director: J. Alexander Poulton
Project Editor: Louise Solomita
Cover Image: photograph by Bruce Bennet/Getty Images Sport

PC: P5

THE TORONTO MAPLE LEAFS

The Stories & Players behind the Legendary Team

J. Alexander Poulton

OVER TIME BOOKS

Contents

Dedication

To all the fans of the Toronto Maple Leafs.

Introduction

Having revealed myself as a Montréal Canadiens fan in my previous books, it was with great trepidation that I approached the task of writing about the Toronto Maple Leafs. After all, I grew up in Montréal, I have been a fan all my life, and my father even worked for the team. Knowing all this, I worried that I would not be able to give an unbiased account of the history of the Toronto club. I slowly came around while reading through the vast amount of literature available on the Leafs; I began to notice that the team's path resembled that of the Montréal Canadiens and that its fans are just as fanatical about the Leafs as Habs fans are about their team.

The Toronto Maple Leafs have been at the forefront of hockey since the team's humble beginnings in the National Hockey Association to today's modern, moneymaking powerhouse. Born out of the ashes of the old National Hockey

Association, the Toronto franchise got its start in the first year of the National Hockey League as the Toronto Arenas in 1917–18. The team got off to a fantastic start, aided by such legends as goaltender Harry "Hap" Holmes and forward Reg Noble. By the end of the regular season, Toronto was in first place overall and headed into the NHL finals against the Montréal Canadiens. The Arenas took the two-game, total-goal series by a final score of 10–7 and moved on to face Pacific Coast Hockey League champs the Vancouver Millionaires for the Stanley Cup. It was a closely contested match, but the Toronto Arenas were up to the challenge and took home their first Stanley Cup.

Toronto would win another Stanley Cup in 1922, but this time they were known as the St. Patricks. The name that would be recognized for countless Stanley Cups and some of the best players in the history of the National Hockey League wasn't adopted until 1927, when Conn Smythe purchased the St. Pats and promptly changed their name to the Toronto Maple Leafs. With stars including Ace Bailey and Hap Day, the Toronto Maple Leafs kept people coming back for more at a time when many NHL teams were struggling to attract new fans. Conn Smythe assured the survival of the franchise when he built Maple Leaf Gardens in 1932 to attract more fans and provide them with a more comfortable atmosphere. The year only got better for the team when it won its first Stanley Cup as the Toronto Maple Leafs. Led by the offensive talents of Charlie Conacher, Joe Primeau and Busher Jackson, nicknamed the "Kid Line," Toronto swept the New York Rangers in the Stanley Cup final and ushered in a new era for the club.

The Maple Leafs remained a competitive team throughout the 1930s but could not repeat as champions. The young club that won the Cup in 1932 was a group of aging veterans by the 1940s, and the team needed a change. Conn Smythe shook up his roster once again, and it paid off almost immediately. New players such as Walter "Turk" Broda, Syl Apps, Sweeney Schriner and Gordie Drillion helped the Maple Leafs to the 1942 Stanley Cup finals, where they won the championship over the Detroit Red Wings in a thrilling seven-game series that saw the Leafs come back from a 3–0 deficit. The decade would only get better for the Leafs as players including Ted Kennedy and Max Bentley joined the team and helped it to three straight Stanley Cups from 1947 to 1949.

Entering the 1950s, many sports pundits had already put the Leafs out to pasture, but the team would prove naysayers wrong in one of the most famous Stanley Cup finals in Toronto history. Toronto and Montréal were well acquainted with one another when they met in finals, and the hatred between the clubs was more than mutual. Each game in the 1951 series went into overtime, and by the time the fifth game came around, the Maple Leafs were up three games to one. The fifth game was again a close affair that needed overtime. It did not take long before Leafs defenceman Bill Barilko snapped in a juicy rebound past Canadiens goaltender Gerry McNeil for the Stanley Cup–winning goal. The Leafs players rushed onto the ice after the goal and hoisted Barilko on their shoulders. But the celebrations would not last long for the Leafs when Barilko disappeared on a fishing trip that summer. What happened to Barilko remained a mystery until 1962, when his body was discovered deep in the Canadian forest where his plane had crashed.

The '50s were a difficult decade for the Leafs, as Detroit and Montréal dominated the regular seasons and the playoffs until the 1960s. Toronto finally found its way out of the basement of the league with the brilliant coaching of Punch Imlach and the stellar performances of such players as Johnny Bower, Tim Horton, George Armstrong, Frank Mahovlich and Red Kelly.

With a lineup that reads like a list of Hall of Fame inductees, the Leafs won another three Stanley Cups in a row from 1962 to 1964. The Leafs were looking for another to add to their collection, but the resurgent Montréal Canadiens put a stop to their hopes of a fourth consecutive Cup. The Leafs would come back just two years later and surprise the hockey world with another Cup victory in 1967. The majority of people had written off the Toronto Maple Leafs in 1967 as a group of over-the-hill veterans with little chance of winning. Goaltender Johnny Bower was in his mid-40s, Red Kelly was in his last season, and their other goaltender, Terry Sawchuk, was past his prime. But the group of veterans together with a few rookies managed to surprise everyone and beat out the Canadiens to win the 1967 Stanley Cup championship.

After the 1967 Stanley Cup victory, things started to turn sour for the Leafs franchise. During the 1970s, Conn Smythe slowly lost control of his beloved team to his son Stafford Smythe and businessman Harold Ballard. The elder Smythe was eventually removed from the decision-making process, and Ballard consolidated his power over the franchise when Stafford Smythe died. Although the club had a few successes in the 1970s, led by Leafs legends Darryl Sittler and Lanny McDonald, Ballard's managerial decisions were slowly sapping the Leafs' spirit, which had taken decades to build. The 1980s was the worst decade for the team's fans. The Leafs remained near the bottom of the league, missed the playoffs on several occasions and looked as though they would never make it back to their earlier winning ways.

But the changes that needed to be made to save the franchise would only come about after the death of Harold Ballard in the 1990s. Cliff Fletcher was put in charge of reorganizing, and by the 1993–94 season, the Leafs were back near the top of the NHL scoring leaders. The Leafs were also making inroads into the playoffs, hoping to make it to the Stanley Cup finals for the first time since 1967, but the hockey gods were not kind to the Leafs and they were eliminated by the Los Angeles Kings just one game away from a berth in the final against rivals the Montréal Canadiens.

Despite a few missteps in recent years, the Leafs have consistently put a quality team on the ice, keeping the hope alive in every fan that the team will bring the Stanley Cup back to Toronto.

Chapter One

Birth of the Blue Dynasty

It is difficult to sort out all the team changes in professional hockey that took place before the formation of the National Hockey Association (NHA), but the city of Toronto has been a centre for the game since the formation of the first leagues in the late 1800s. After a few unsuccessful attempts to form a winning team in the city, hockey fans could finally show pride in the local Toronto Blueshirts, who were granted a franchise in the NHA in 1912. After a few unsuccessful years and numerous ownership changes, the Blueshirts fell into the hands of businessman Eddie Livingstone. This change in ownership of one team would alter the course of professional hockey forever.

During World War I, it was difficult for most teams to find enough quality players to put on the ice come game time. Luckily for the Toronto team, Livingstone was quite adept at finding loopholes in the league's system to secure the better players for his team. When the rival Pacific Coast Hockey Association(PCHA) persuaded a chunk of the Toronto Blueshirts to leave the NHA with the promise of more money, however, Livingstone was left with the prospect of not having a team at the start of the 1915–16 season. Luckily, Livingstone also owned another Toronto NHA franchise, the Ontarios. He simply transferred the players from the Ontarios to the Blueshirts and folded the first club. But the slickness with which he conducted his business rubbed other team owners the wrong way, and Livingstone made a few enemies. Chief among Livingstone's detractors was Montréal Wanderers owner Sam Lichtenhein.

Lichtenhein was further angered when, during a regular-season game, Toronto's Ken Randall slammed the Wanderers' star player, Sprague Cleghorn, into the boards. Randall skated away from the collision, but Cleghorn was left on the ice with a fractured ankle and torn ligaments. To add insult to injury, Cleghorn was such a vital part of the Wanderers' success that, though they were at the top of the league before his injury, they fell to 3–13 for the remaining games of the season.

The other owners' ire was further raised when Livingstone reacquired Frank Foyston and Harry Holmes, whom he had lost to the PCHA, in the middle of the season. What bothered the owners was that Livingstone was only able to get the two star players back because when they jumped to the PCHA, they were not put on suspension in the NHA as would normally have occurred. Although the additional players did not help the Toronto Blueshirts, who didn't make it into the Stanley Cup final that year, the other owners were still angered by the underhanded way Livingstone secured an advantage.

Things only got worse between Livingstone and the other owners. After a few trade disputes and arguments over how the Stanley Cup playoffs would be structured, the owners of the Montréal Canadiens, Québec Bulldogs, Montréal Wanderers and Ottawa Senators got together and plotted to get rid of Livingstone.

During the 1916–17 season, the NHA added another Toronto team to the schedule, made up of players from the Canadian Military's 228th Battalion. The team was extremely popular with local crowds, but their future in the league was uncertain given that they could be called to active duty at any moment and get shipped off to Europe. The 228th Battalion managed to finish the first half of the season in a respectable second place behind the Montréal Canadiens. But the need for soldiers grew too great for the military to allow the battalion to continue playing, and they were recalled halfway through the season. When the other owners met to decide how to proceed with the rest of the year, they took the opportunity to dump the unpopular Livingstone and his Toronto Blueshirts from the league without any compensation.

Livingstone tried in vain to get himself back in with the NHA, but the owners had blocked all legal loopholes. To permanently remove any possibility of Livingstone getting his foot back in the league, the remaining teams met in November 1917 and decided to form a new league. The Québec Bulldogs, who could not pull enough players together to form a team in time, were forced to remove themselves. This left the new league with two teams from Montreal and one from Ottawa. If the new league was going to survive as a proper representation of Eastern Canadian hockey, it would need more than two cities. With Livingstone safely on the outside, it was decided that Toronto needed to have a team to secure the new league's success.

On November 26, 1917, all interested parties finally came to an agreement and the National Hockey League(NHL) was formed. Frank Calder, former NHA secretary-treasurer, was named the NHL's first president. The new league had four teams to begin operations, the two Montréal teams, a team from Ottawa, and a new Toronto franchise headed by a select group of approved Toronto businessmen.

"The new owners were thoroughly acceptable," said Calder, obviously referring to the previous rift with Livingstone.

The team that would eventually become the Toronto Maple Leafs officially began operations as the Toronto Arenas on December 19, 1917, losing its first game against the Montréal Wanderers by a score of 10–9. (The club was not formally named the Arenas until the following season.)

With players like Reg Noble, Alf Skinner and goaltender Hap Holmes, the Arenas finished their first season tied with the Montréal Canadiens and in a good spot to challenge for the Stanley Cup.

In a closely contested NHL final, Toronto came out victorious in a two-game total-goal series against the Canadiens, winning 10–7. This earned Toronto the right to challenge the PCHA champion Vancouver Millionaires for the Stanley Cup. Before 1926, when the Stanley Cup became property of the National Hockey League, the winners from the NHL and PCHA leagues would play each other for the right to call themselves Stanley Cup champions.

The series between the Vancouver Millionaires and the Toronto Arenas went the full five games, with Toronto eking out a 2–1 victory in the final game to win the first Stanley Cup for an NHL franchise. Alf Skinner was the Arenas' standout player of the Stanley Cup finals, scoring 8 goals, while Arenas goaltender Hap Holmes shut down the Millionaires' offence with some spectacular saves.

Toronto's fortunes would turn dramatically after their inaugural Stanley Cup championship season in the NHL. The Arenas finished off the 1918–19 season, which lasted 18 games, with a dismal record of 5 wins and 13 losses. After the Arenas' meteoric rise to the top in the first year and their fall from grace the next season, several of the franchise's owners sold their shares to other investors.

Also because of its dismal season, the club was having trouble attracting a crowd for the large, 8000-seat arena, so before the start of the next season, the new Toronto owners decided a name change was in order to attract fans. At that time in Toronto, the Irish made up a considerable portion of the city's population, so to bring them out to games, the team was renamed the Toronto St. Patricks (St. Pats for short).

Under new management, the St. Pats improved their record during the 1919–20 season, but the Ottawa Senators proved too strong for any team that season and walked away with the Stanley Cup. In 1920–21, the St. Pats added the services of scoring ace Babe Dye from the Hamilton Tigers and the tough defensive skills of Sprague Cleghorn, helping Toronto finish the second half of the regular season with a league-leading record of 10–4.

In the NHL finals, the St. Pats were no match for the high-powered offence of the Ottawa Senators in their two-game total-goal series, and Toronto lost by a score of 7–0. There was no doubt that the St. Pats had the goal-scoring touch to challenge the Senators, but they had not counted on Senators goaltender Clint Benedict coming up with one of the best playoff performances of his career. Toronto's weakness was in goal, and during the off-season the team replaced goaltender Jack Forbes with John Ross Roach. With that change, the St. Pats' fortunes immediately turned around.

While the Montréal Canadiens and the Hamilton Tigers floundered during the 1921–22 regular season, the Senators and the St. Pats took full advantage and easily walked into another NHL final against each other to fight for the right to battle for the ultimate prize, the Stanley Cup.

Even though it was a two-game total-goal series, the victor was decided in the first game with Toronto coming out on the winning end, amassing 5 goals to Ottawa's 4. The Senators needed only 2 goals and an amazing performance from reliable goaltender Clint Benedict to move on to the Stanley Cup final. The St. Pats' defence shut down the Senators' top scorers, including Punch Broadbent, who led the regular season in scoring, Cy Denneny and Frank Nighbor. St. Pats goaltender John Ross Roach held the fort in the second game with the kind of performance that could have kept the St. Pats in the playoffs the previous year. It wasn't an easy game for either side, since the unseasonably warm weather left huge puddles of water all over the natural ice surface at Ottawa's Day Arena. (That was the last time an NHL game was played on natural ice.) Despite the hardships, Toronto prevailed and moved on to the next challenge.

Roach's stellar rookie performance continued into the Stanley Cup final against the Vancouver Millionaires. Roach and the rest of the Toronto squad looked a little shaky in the first game of the series (which was held entirely in Toronto), losing the game 4–3. But for the second game, Toronto tightened up its defence and managed to win 2–1 after a tense overtime period.

The Millionaires could not seem to match Toronto's pace in the series, even though they won the third game 3–0. The St. Pats just wanted to win more, and they were carried through games four and five on the strength of Roach's performance—he recorded the first shutout in Stanley Cup play by an NHL rookie, achieving the feat in game four with a 6–0 victory. Roach continued to dominate into the final game while his teammates buried Vancouver to finish off the series with a 5–1 victory. Toronto's Babe Dye was the star forward of the playoffs, scoring 9 goals in 5 games. After only five years in the NHL, Toronto had two Stanley Cups under its belt and had won over the fans and the city.

Although the club did not win another Stanley Cup as the St. Pats, Toronto fans continued to support the team. They came out in record numbers to watch the likes of Cecil "Babe" Dye, the fiery "Jolly" Jack Adams and the consistent Reg Noble.

Babe Dye was an extraordinary athlete. He played halfback for the Toronto Argonauts when he wasn't on the ice, and during the summer he could be found at the baseball diamond in the outfield for teams in Baltimore, Buffalo and Toronto. Dye enjoyed these other pursuits, but his passion was for the game of hockey. At just 5'8" and 150 pounds, Dye could not rely on his physical presence to score his many goals, so he called upon his incredible stick handling, blistering shot and near-perfect accuracy. Maple Leafs legend King Clancy, then playing for the Ottawa Senators, could vouch for Dye's shooting effectiveness.

"Babe had the most deadly shot in the NHL. He wasn't a really good skater, but he could blast that puck like dynamite and he was a terrific competitor," Clancy said.

During the 1924–25 season, Dye led the league in scoring with 38 goals and 8 assists for 46 points. His 38 goals stood as a franchise record until 35 years later, when Frank Mahovlich broke the record with 48 goals. Dye continued to be a force within the St. Pats organization until the 1926–27 season, when he was sold to the Chicago Blackhawks.

"Jolly" Jack Adams joined the Toronto organization in 1917–18 and promptly won his first Stanley Cup. He played another season for Toronto before being lured out west to play with the Vancouver Millionaires, but he would eventually return to Toronto in 1922 to reclaim his

place with the St. Pats. Adams was a regular con-
tributor to the St. Pats' offence, finishing all but
one year just behind Babe Dye in team scoring.
While Dye relied on his stick-handling abilities
and accurate shot to score goals, Adams' speed
helped him in puck races and put him in position
for a quick shot on net. With Noble rounding out
the line, the trio formed one of the deadliest
combinations in the early days of hockey.

Reg Noble was the most consistent player on
the St. Pats squad. The Toronto captain had been
playing for the team since the beginning and
remained with them until 1924–25, playing both
forward and defensive positions. His reliability at
both ends of the ice contributed to Toronto's
early success and to his line's offensive production. The same year the Toronto Arenas won the
first Stanley Cup in NHL history, Reg Noble
scored 30 goals and 10 assists to finish third
overall in scoring behind the Canadiens' Joe
Malone and Ottawa's Cy Denneny.

Sportswriter Lou Marsh described Noble's
outstanding style after the St. Pats' 1922 Cup
victory: "The work of Captain Reg Noble at
centre was by far his best effort of the season and
bulked big in the St. Pats' success. He showed
plenty of hockey north of his shoulder blades.
He swung his stick as long as a bass rod and he

broke up play after play in the goulash area in mid-ice."

By the 1925–26 season, Toronto went from being one of the top teams in the league to one of the worst. By the start of the 1926–27 season, the group that owned the St. Pats was considering selling the team to another city.

Meanwhile, in the expanded NHL, the New York Rangers were busy assembling a team for the start of the new season. Of all the players available, Toronto's Babe Dye was who everyone wanted. Rangers general manager Conn Smythe did not think the veteran player had many good years left in him, so he decided to pass on picking him up. Rangers owner Colonel Hammond was so upset that Smythe hadn't so much as called to express interest in Dye that he immediately fired Smythe and replaced him with Lester Patrick.

Without a place to call his own, Smythe convinced the Toronto franchise owners to keep the club in the city and sell the team to him for $160,000. In February of 1927, the most important deal in Toronto hockey history was made when the keys to the Mutual Street Arena were handed over to Conn Smythe.

Not wasting any time to make his mark, Smythe made two changes that would alter the team's history. On February 15, the club was renamed the Toronto Maple Leafs (after the World War I Canadian Maple Leaf Regiment), and the team's uniform was changed from the green and white of the St. Pats to the blue and white of the Leafs. In the first game played as the Maple Leafs on February 17, 1927, Toronto won 4–1 over the New York Americans.

Although the Leafs ended the season at the bottom of the Canadian division, with each passing year they steadily climbed up the points ladder and began attracting larger and larger crowds.

Chapter Two

The House that Conn Smythe Built

With Smythe at the helm and his knowledgeable assistant Frank Selke by his side, the Toronto Maple Leafs began the task of reconstructing the franchise. The cornerstones of the new Leafs were none other than legends Irvin "Ace" Bailey and Clarence "Happy" Day.

Bailey finished the 1928–29 season as the Leafs' top scorer, helping his team out of the league's cellar and up to a spot in the playoffs for the first time since 1925. The Leafs also began to pay more attention to their farm system and to developing players who would ensure the club's success not only in the present but also during decades to come. By the start of the 1929–30 season, a new wave of young players began to make a mark on the club. Three rookies stood out as the future of the Toronto franchise: Charlie Conacher, Joe Primeau and Harvey "Busher" Jackson would form one of the most potent offensive lines of the '30s (nicknamed the "Kid Line") and change the Maple Leafs' fortunes for the better.

By the 1930–31 season, the Toronto Maple Leafs were one of the elite teams in the league. Charlie "the Big Bomber" Conacher, at 6'1" and 195 pounds, was not a player to be taken lightly. His shot—one of the hardest in hockey at that time—made goaltenders cringe and put a number of dents in boards around the league. The first Maple Leafs star to have been raised in the city of Toronto itself, Conacher quickly became a fan favourite. Using his size to his advantage, he placed himself in the right spot to receive many of those precision passes his linemate Joe Primeau became known for. Although they did not win the Cup that season, Toronto fans were not disappointed by their team's performance and knew that with a good mix of young talent and veteran know-how they could give teams like the Montréal Canadiens a run for their money.

Along with the youth, Conn Smythe rounded out his squad by acquiring the veteran talent of Francis Michael Clancy, more commonly known as King Clancy. Clancy wasn't known for his goal-scoring ability, but he did have the things a team of young players most needed:

leadership, a competitive spirit and what he had most of all—charisma.

At 5'7" and 155 pounds, Clancy was not the most imposing figure on the Leafs squad, but his work ethic was unquestionable. He could skate like the wind, and the star was continually back-checking, endearing himself to his goaltenders and defencemen. With the right ingredients in place, the Toronto Maple Leafs became the biggest draw in town.

There was just one problem with the increased demand for tickets. The old Mutual Street Arena—or Arena Gardens, as it was more commonly known—the home of the Toronto's NHL franchise since 1917, had seen better days and could not accommodate the number of people who now wanted to get in to see the games. Conn Smythe knew that a new arena had to be built in order for the Leafs to survive. Smythe envisioned a grand hockey palace that would be the envy of all the other teams in the league, but a few obstacles stood in his way before he could break any ground.

Smythe had a new arena in mind even when he first purchased the Toronto franchise, and with the team's recent success on the ice he felt confident in moving ahead. He started gathering the financial support he needed in 1930 and

then began the difficult task of finding a loca-
tion. He considered several sites, including one
at the corner of Yonge and Fleet streets, but
finally settled upon one that was bordered by
Carlton, Wood, and Church streets. The same
architectural firm that designed Toronto's Union
Station was selected to build the new arena, and
on June 1, 1931, construction began on Maple
Leaf Gardens. Smythe wanted the building ready
for the opening game of the 1931–32 season, and
pushed the construction crew to get it done as
fast as they could. The concrete had barely dried
when just 166 days later, on November 12, 1931,
Maple Leaf Gardens was complete and ready to
host its first NHL game. A capacity crowd of
13,542 fans jammed into the new arena to see
their team play the Chicago Blackhawks. Fans
left the Gardens a little disappointed, however, .
as their team fell 2–1 in a rather uneventful
game. Chicago's Harold "Mush" Marsh had the
distinction of scoring the first goal in Maple Leaf
Gardens when he fired a shot past Lorne Chabot
at 2 minutes and 30 seconds of the first period.

Maple Leaf Gardens wasn't just your ordinary
local arena with bathrooms and concession
stands. Smythe had a poolroom installed along
with a gymnasium and bowling alley. He even
had cats roaming the Gardens freely to ensure
that any rodents would quickly be taken care of.

Smythe spared no expense when it came to providing for his team and the fans. Maple Leaf Gardens was the first NHL arena to have a four-faced clock that everyone in the arena could see, the first to use a goal judge and the first to use penalty clocks.

With his house now in order, Smythe needed a good season to ensure fans would keep coming back. He had no idea what his team was about to accomplish.

Chapter Three

The Toronto Maple Leafs' First Stanley Cup

Before opening a new season and a new building, Conn Smythe knew he needed to add one more ingredient to his team that would make it a true Stanley Cup contender. Smythe was not happy with coach Art Duncan after the team bowed out of the playoffs against the Chicago Blackhawks in the 1931 quarterfinals. Smythe wanted a character like himself behind the bench, someone who would speak his mind and not shy away from dismantling a player if he wasn't playing up to team standards. Smythe found all these qualities in Dick Irvin.

As a player, Dick Irvin was known for his work ethic and his ability to put the puck in the net. But when a fractured skull forced him to hang up his skates, Irvin could not tear himself away from the game and was offered the position of head coach for his old team, the Chicago Blackhawks. Coaching in his first full year with the

Blackhawks, Irvin took his team all the way to the Stanley Cup finals only to lose to the Montréal Canadiens in the final game.

When Smythe learned that Irvin had been cut loose by the Chicago Blackhawks before the start of the 1931–32 season, he knew he could get the coach he wanted for his Leafs. A few games into that season, Smythe had had enough with Art Duncan. Smythe phoned Irvin in Chicago and asked him to coach in Toronto; Irvin accepted and took his place behind the bench on November 28, 1931.

To make the new coach's transition to the team a little easier and to give Irvin more time to get to know the players, Smythe took the coaching reins for the first game while Irvin sat on the sidelines and observed. The idea was to ease Irvin slowly into his coaching job, but when the Boston Bruins came back to tie the game 4–4, Smythe turned to Irvin and handed him the job. The tied game ended up going into overtime, with the Leafs winning 6–5.

Once he was at the helm, Irvin set about making a few changes that would make his good players great.

Irvin knew he had a good team to work with, but they lacked the work ethic and discipline that could make them Stanley Cup champions. Irvin put his team through strenuous workouts and constant practices, stressing that the players stick to a disciplined, systematic game. Irvin knew that if they played as a team and stuck to the system, they could be the best in the NHL. Everything appeared to be going according to Irvin's plan as the Leafs took over first place in the Canadian Division on December 22 after a 9–3 victory over the New York Americans.

Although the "Kid Line" of Charlie Conacher, Joe Primeau and Busher Jackson was responsible for the majority of the scoring, Irvin was getting a well-rounded effort from the rest of the team. Hap Day, Harold Darragh and King Clancy provided the Leafs with the defence they needed, making them tough to beat every time they hit the ice.

Conn Smythe continued to smile as the season progressed and his team drew large crowds to the Maple Leaf Gardens, with gross ticket revenues that had never been seen at the old Mutual Street Arena. As the season continued and the Toronto Maple Leafs remained in a head-to-head battle with the Montréal Canadiens for first place in the Canadian Division, interest in the Toronto team just kept growing. This was a surprise to many during a time when other teams around the league were struggling because of the Depression. The Leafs regularly had a full house, and on the days when the Montréal Canadiens came to town, the Gardens was completely sold out.

In one game on February 13, 1932, the Maple Leafs trounced the Canadiens in a 6–0 victory that saw nine major penalties handed out after a free-for-all fight. Several players were fined $25 by NHL president Frank Calder for their involvement in the fracas. The rough play as teams fought for a spot in the playoffs continued into the last few games of the season. Even Conn Smythe got involved in some on-ice action.

On March 15, 1932, the Leafs were in Boston with just four games remaining in the regular season and were in a heated race with the Canadiens for first place in the Canadian division. Every win counted, and the Leafs general manager placed himself behind the bench for the remaining games to ensure his team was playing its best. But the Leafs were not doing very well against the Bruins that night, and Smythe quickly lost his temper when, with the score tied, Toronto goaltender Lorne Chabot tripped Boston's Cooney Weiland as he passed by Chabot's net. Referee Bill Stewart spotted the infraction and gave Chabot a two-minute penalty. While Chabot was in the box, the Bruins managed to put three goals past the defencemen left in charge of guarding the net (at that time, goaltenders had to serve their own penalties). After the third goal was scored, Conn Smythe's face turned bright red. Fuming over the injustice, Smythe grabbed the referee by the sweater as he skated by the Toronto bench and berated him for Chabot's penalty. The referee then ordered Smythe to leave his spot behind the bench, and when Smythe refused, arena attendants were called to physically remove him. Seeing their manager being forcefully removed, several players joined in the melee. More players and attendants began to join the fight, and Boston Bruins president Charles Adams had to bring in the police to restore order. Conn Smythe had the last word in the end, retaking his spot behind Toronto's bench for the rest of the game. The Leafs lost by a final score of 6–2.

Toronto finished the season just behind the Montréal Canadiens in their division and third overall in the league, only one point behind the Rangers. Busher Jackson and Joe Primeau finished at the top of the scoring race while their linemate Charlie Conacher tied the Rangers' Bill Cook for leading goal scorer.

Toronto started its playoff run on March 27, 1932, in Chicago, taking on the Blackhawks in a rematch of the previous year's quarterfinals. Having coached in Chicago, Dick Irvin knew very well what his team had to do to defeat the Hawks. Irvin knew that if his scoring lines could break Chicago's defensive wall and get a few pucks past Vezina Trophy–winning goaltender Charlie Gardiner, then the Leafs could easily run away with the series. The Hawks were not much of a threat on offence, having scored only 86 goals during the regular season compared to the Leafs' 155. The defensive duo of Clarence "Taffy" Abel and Marvin "Cyclone" Wentworth had kept forwards out of their zone all season long, and the Hawks didn't changed their tactics for the first game against Toronto.

Chicago's tight defensive style continually frustrated the Leafs' sharpshooters, and when they did manage a shot on net, they could put nothing by the superb Gardiner. Lorne Chabot was doing his part to keep his team in the game by making some brilliant saves, but the Leafs were simply out-worked, and it was only a matter of time before the Hawks put one in. Gerry Lowrey, who managed to score only 8 goals during the regular season, scored the game-winning goal in the third period, ending the match with a less-than-exciting 1–0 victory.

The second and final game of the total-goal series was a completely different affair. Chicago waltzed into Maple Leaf Gardens, confident that their defensive system could handle anything the speedy Leafs forwards could throw at them and certain that if Toronto got around their defence, they always could rely on Gardiner to keep them in the game.

The Gardens was filled to capacity with eager fans hoping for some sweet retribution against the team that eliminated them in the last year's playoffs. Irving made a few minor adjustments to compensate for the defensive system of the Hawks and found that his players responded well. The fans who packed the Gardens stood for almost the entire game as they watched their Leafs trounce the Hawks in a 6–1 rout. Charlie Conacher was the star of the game with 2 goals. The Gardens roared with approval as the Leafs exacted their revenge on the Hawks and earned a spot in the next round against the Montréal Maroons.

The Maple Leafs were the favourites in the semifinals against the Maroons, but with veteran talent including Nels Stewart and Lionel Conacher (Charlie's brother), the Leafs knew they could not take their opponents for granted. It was a tough defensive game in Montréal with neither team dominating. Charlie Conacher got the first goal after stick-handling his way past brother Lionel and putting a fancy move on goaltender Flat Walsh. The Maroons evened up the score late in the third period when Dave Trottier put in the tying goal.

The second game was held in Toronto before a record crowd of 14,000 eager fans. Irvin drilled his players before the game, hoping to make them understand that if they stuck to the system that got them past the Blackhawks, they would have no problem making it past the Maroons.

The Leafs looked a little nervous as they made their way through the first moments of the first period. Even a goal by the Leafs' Red Horner could not get rid of their nerves as the Maroons came back with 2 goals of their own by Jimmy Ward and Babe Siebert and carried that lead well into the third period. Every time the Leafs would get the puck, the Maroons would be at their heels trying to take it away or dump it back into the Leafs zone. With little time remaining in the game, the fans at the Gardens got to their feet and lifted the roof with the roar from the stands. The Leafs were all standing on the bench, screaming words of support at their teammates on the ice, intensifying the atmosphere in the Gardens.

A hush fell as Hap Day broke away with the puck on an individual rush toward Maroons goaltender Flat Walsh. The fans held their collective breath as Day made his move on Walsh from in close and put the puck in the net to tie the game. The crowd exploded, cheering for Toronto's captain for three straight minutes. Neither team could put in another goal to break the tie before the third period ended, sending the game into sudden-death overtime.

Both teams were apprehensive in the first few minutes of the overtime period, not wanting to open up any opportunities for the other, but Irvin kept up the pressure on his players to push forward and take the risks needed to win the series and make it to the finals. He knew that if the Maroons broke into the Leafs' zone, he had one of the best goaltenders in Lorne Chabot to stop whatever the Maroons could produce. At the 18th minute of the first overtime period, the Leafs' Bob Gracie finally broke the deadlock, putting a shot past Flat Walsh for the victory. The Gardens erupted as the Leafs cleared their bench and swarmed Gracie. Toronto was on to the next stage to face the New York Rangers for the Cup.

Although the Rangers finished the regular season with more points than the Leafs and had a week off before the start of the finals, they looked shaky in the opening game of the series. Former Leafs goaltender John Ross Roach looked unsteady before his home crowd of about 16,000 screaming Rangers fans. Both goaltenders' jobs were made all the more difficult as the game was rife with penalties—some 20 were dealt out to both teams by the end of the game. But when the smoke cleared, the Maple Leafs were the victors with a 6–4 score. Busher Jackson was the star for Toronto, scoring a hat trick.

In what can be viewed as a sign of how much hockey mattered to American audiences in the early days, game two of the Stanley Cup finals had to be moved out of Madison Square Garden to Boston Garden because of a scheduling conflict with a circus. Despite the fact that the Bruins weren't playing in the final, 12,000 die-hard Boston hockey fans still showed up to see the Rangers and the Leafs play. The Rangers quickly secured themselves a 2-goal lead but completely fell apart later in the game when King Clancy and Charlie Conacher potted 2 goals each. John Ross Roach just was not playing the way he had against the Montréal Canadiens in the Rangers' first series, and he let in another 6 goals. The game ended with the Leafs scoring six and the Rangers only two. The Rangers were now on the verge of losing the Cup in the best-of-five series. Back in Toronto in front of their hometown fans, the Leafs were confident they could end the series with a strong performance.

Before a capacity crowd of 14,366 at the Maple Leaf Gardens, the Leafs played a great game of hockey. They controlled most of the game despite the hat trick by Rangers forward Frank Boucher. John Ross Roach was again the difference in the game, looking like a nervous rookie in the Rangers net and letting in a number of easy shots. When the final buzzer sounded, Toronto had won the game and their first Stanley Cup as the Maple Leafs. The "Gashouse Gang," as the Leafs had come to be known, had electrified the city with their Cup win and continued to dominate the National Hockey League as the decade went on.

Chapter Four

Disappointing Success

The next several years were trying times for Toronto Maple Leafs fans. The Leafs remained one of the top teams in the National Hockey League for much of the 1930s, but they could never get anywhere in the playoffs. But in the 1932–33 regular season, the Maple Leafs finished at the top of the Canadian Division and had one of that year's most exciting playoff runs to get into the Stanley Cup finals.

The Boston Bruins came back in 1932–33 after a horrible season the year before. Boston goaltender Tiny Thompson returned to form with a 1.76 goals-against average and defenceman Eddie Shore was back at the top of his game, taking home the most valuable player award for his efforts. Toronto had a skilled team to face off against the Bruins in the semifinals, but sportswriters predicted the series would go to the Boston team.

The best-of-five series started in Boston, to the dismay of the Leafs, who had not won a game there since 1929. Game one was a rough-and-tumble affair, with equal chances on goal for both teams. If the performances of Toronto goaltender Lorne Chabot and the Bruins' Tiny Thompson were any indication of how the series was to progress, then fans were in for some nail-biting hockey. Even the crowd in Boston got into the action. As the teams filed off the ice at the end of the second period, one fan attacked Toronto's Ace Bailey. Luckily for the irate fan, arena attendants quickly intervened, preventing Bailey from teaching the agitator a painful lesson. By the end of the third period of game one, both goaltenders had turned away all but one shot, forcing overtime. Dit Clapper scored the only goal in regulation time for the Bruins, and Bill Thoms had the only goal for the Maple Leafs.

The pressure on the goaltenders did not let up in the overtime period, but Thompson and Chabot were well up to the task; it was just a matter of who would break first. The game could not last forever, and luckily for the fans in Boston, it was their own Marty Barry who caught a pass from Dit Clapper and put one in past Lorne Chabot at 14:14 of the first overtime period to take the first game away from the Leafs.

Boston fans were privileged to witness another tight, physical matchup in game two with some excellent goaltending on both sides by Chabot and Thompson. The goaltenders made one miraculous save after another, keeping high-scoring forwards like the Bruins' Marty Barry and the Leafs' Charlie Conacher off the score sheet. The game would need another overtime period before one team could come away the victor. This time it was the Leafs who caught a break when the Bruins' Georges Owen was sent to the penalty box for tripping Bill Thoms. On the ensuing power play, Busher Jackson took a pass from Thoms and put the puck behind goaltender Thompson. The Boston Garden quieted down as fans headed for the exits, disappointed that the Bruins could not take a commanding lead in the series. With the series all tied up, the teams packed up their gear and headed to Toronto.

With predictions of an easy Boston win gone completely out the window, everyone expected game three to be another nail-biter—and it was. Boston's Nels Stewart put his team up early in the game off a beautiful pass from Eddie Shore. Toronto could not find the back of the net until late in the third period, when Ken Doraty finally put a puck past Thompson to tie the game and once again force overtime. It took the Bruins just over four minutes to end the game when

Eddie Shore broke through Toronto's defence and found a clear path to Chabot. Shore made a simple move with his stick and put the puck past the goalie, much to the displeasure of the Toronto fans and players.

On the verge of elimination from the playoffs, Toronto players made their coach proud in game four when they pounded the Bruins 5–3 in a very physical confrontation. This left one game to decide who would go on to play in the Stanley Cup finals.

Fans could not ask for anything more from two hockey teams. Boston and Toronto were playing physical games with plenty of opportunities on goal. Both goaltenders were playing some of the best hockey of their careers, making for some close, tense games. The 14,000 fans lucky enough to get a ticket to the final game of the series had no idea they were in for one of the most suspense-filled games of them all.

Much to the delight of the hometown Toronto crowd, the Leafs started out the game on the offensive with the "Kid Line" of Busher Jackson, Charlie Conacher and Joe Primeau leading the attacks on the Bruins net. After his poor performance in game four, Cecil "Tiny" Thompson returned to his Vezina Trophy–winning ways and stopped everything the Leafs threw at him with some spectacular saves. Boston regrouped for the start of the second period and put constant pressure on the Leafs' defence. Led by forwards Nels Stewart and Marty Barry, and the pinpoint passing of Eddie Shore, Toronto goaltender Lorne Chabot had to be sharp on every shot. Toronto mounted a stingy defence with rear guards Red Horner, Hap Day and the back-checking King Clancy keeping the frustrated Bruins at bay. Throughout the second and third periods, the fans were treated to some of the best hockey they had seen in the Gardens all year, but neither team could put the puck in the net. As the buzzer sounded the end of regulation time, there was a sense in the building that the game might go on forever.

The first overtime period started with neither side willing to take a chance on the offence. There was some hard hitting and a few chances on goal, but the first overtime was played mostly in the neutral zone.

When nothing changed after the second, third, fourth, and fifth overtime periods, the fans who were still awake wondered if they would make it home before sunrise. If it was difficult for the fans, it was almost impossible for the players. On both benches, players were taking shorter shifts and moving a lot slower than at the beginning of the game. National Hockey League president Frank Calder was in attendance and like every one else, he was getting a little worried that the game might never end. During the intermission following the fifth overtime period, Calder approached the referees with a few radical ideas on how to bring the game to a close. He rejected the suggestion that the game be stopped and started again on another day because the winner had to be in New York the next day for the start of the finals, but he did entertain the idea of removing the goaltenders. That notion was quickly shot down because the winner would be whoever got the first shot on net. Calder must have been a gambling man because his next suggestion was to decide the winner by the toss of a coin. But when it was announced that the game would be decided this way, 14,000 fans booed the idea mercilessly until the lengthy showdown was allowed to proceed into the sixth overtime period.

Luckily, it didn't take much longer for the game to be decided. At 1:50 a.m., just four minutes into the sixth overtime, Toronto's Ken Doraty took a pass from Andy Blair, skated past the weary Boston defence, and poked the puck past Tiny Thompson for the game- and series-winning goal.

Toronto went on to face the Rangers for the Stanley Cup but lost in four games to the well-rested New York team. Despite this defeat, things were still looking bright for the Maple Leafs. They were simply too tired to play effective hockey against the Rangers, and their fans knew they would be back the next season to challenge for the Cup again.

Although the Leafs spent the majority of the 1930s at the top of the league, each year brought a new disappointment that kept them from hoisting the Stanley Cup. The 1933–34 season brought the team a challenge no one had expected.

A few weeks into the new season, the Leafs were once again at the top of the league, riding high on the success of their young players. As much as they relied on the young guys to score, it was the veteran players who rounded out the team and made them a complete unit, and none was more instrumental than longtime Leaf Irvin "Ace" Bailey.

In his younger days, Bailey was always a top scorer for the Leafs, but in recent seasons, his goal production had slowed. Although he was no longer the electrifying player he had been a few years before, Bailey was still a favourite of fans in Toronto. But the veteran player's career took a sudden turn for the worse just 13 games into the season on December 12, 1933, during a game against the Boston Bruins.

Since joining the league in 1926, Boston's Eddie Shore was well known for playing a tough style of defence. He was notorious around the league for his robust game and his propensity for dishing out punishing checks. On that December night in Boston after a rough first period, the score was deadlocked at one apiece. Eddie Shore was particularly active that night, hitting players in his usual unfriendly manner. Wanting to give Shore a taste of his own medicine, King Clancy tripped Shore from behind as he skated out of the Toronto zone. When referee Odie Cleghorn failed to call a penalty on the play, Shore immediately jumped to his feet and looked for the Leafs player in order to exact his revenge. Accounts vary of what occurred next, but the consensus is that after Shore jumped to his feet, he either mistook Bailey for Clancy or simply went after the closest Leafs player. Seething with rage, Shore viciously checked Bailey from behind, sending him flying. As Bailey landed, his unprotected head hit the ice, and he was knocked out cold. Bailey's fellow players screamed for a doctor as they watched in horror while their teammate's body twitched on the cold ice. As the players huddled around Bailey, Toronto defenceman

Red Horner was livid that Shore was showing no remorse. After exchanging a few unpleasant words with Shore, Horner punched him in the jaw, sending the Bruins defenceman to the ice. As the commotion began to subside, Bailey and Shore were taken to their dressing rooms for medical attention. It took a while for the play to resume but by the end of the game, the Leafs came out the victors with a 4–1 win. Once the play stopped, however, the action continued unabated off the ice.

As crowds lined the corridors leading to the dressing rooms, fists began to fly as people tussled to get closer. Conn Smythe was trying to get into the Leafs' dressing room through the masses when a fan tried to stop him from going in. Without any hesitation, Smythe punched the fan in his way, knocking him to the ground. Smythe was later hauled into court on assault charges, but the judge dismissed the case because he deemed that Smythe was under extreme stress at the time.

As for Bailey, he was rushed to hospital where a team of neurosurgeons performed two operations to repair his broken skull and remove two blood clots. After he was out of critical condition, Bailey returned to Toronto to continue his rehabilitation. As word of his recovery began to spread, the NHL decided to suspend Shore for

16 games. Upon leaving hospital, Bailey told the media he wanted to make a full return to the league, but his injuries were deemed too severe for him to risk another head trauma.

Furious at the penalty handed out to Shore, Smythe went before the NHL board of governors in an attempt to get a stiffer suspension for the Bruins tough guy, but Smythe was shot down. The NHL settled on a benefit game for Bailey in which all the proceeds would go to paying hospital bills and for Bailey's lost revenue. The game would be held at the Maple Leaf Gardens between the Leafs and a collection of the NHL's top players.

On February 14, 1934, the Maple Leaf Gardens was crowded with over 14,000 people eager to watch a game that would benefit one of their favourite players. The NHL all-stars appeared in orange and black uniforms, and the Toronto players wore blue with the word "ACE" written across their jerseys. There was tension in the air as the pre-game ceremony started because among the invited top NHLers was Boston Bruins defenceman Eddie Shore. Ace Bailey walked out to centre ice to thunderous applause and shook the hand of each player. The crowd went silent as Eddie Shore skated up to Bailey and extended his hand. As Bailey accepted the peace offering, the crowd erupted in applause.

The Leafs won the game 7–3 and collected about $30,000 for Bailey and his family. After the game, reporters circled around Bailey, asking him how he felt about shaking hands with the man who took him out of the game he loved.

"I was never the type of man to hold grudges against anybody," Bailey said.

Despite the loss of one of their veteran players, the Leafs continued their successful season, finished atop the league in points and were favourites to make it into the finals. But things did not go well in the playoffs for the Maple Leafs, who lost to the Detroit Red Wings in the 1934 semifinals and continued to disappoint fans throughout the '30s. The team finished the 1934–35 season again at the top of the NHL, but they lost in three straight games to the Montréal Maroons in the Stanley Cup finals. It was the same story in the 1936 Cup finals, when the Red Wings defeated the Leafs in four games. The Leafs' management could do nothing to explain the team's post-season mistakes. Some sportswriters said the Leafs' top scorers did not step up in the important games and that there was too much reliance on centre Joe Primeau. But when a team is not doing well in the playoffs, the eventual blame almost certainly falls on the coach. Many critics said that Irvin wasn't tough enough on his players when it came to the big games and that after several seasons of early exits from the playoffs, the players had lost confidence in their bench boss. Soon, Irvin came to the conclusion that his time with the Maple Leafs had run its course and that after the 1939–40 season, he would leave his post as coach. Conn Smythe accepted his resignation, and after the Leafs lost another Stanley Cup final to the New York Rangers on April 13, 1940, Irvin had coached his last game for the team.

Chapter Five

A New Hope

While the Leafs didn't win another championship in the 1930s, they played great hockey during the regular season and built up a solid base of young players to take them into the next decade.

In the late 1930s, the links to the farm system that Frank Selke had built up over the decade began to pay off. Players such as Syl Apps, Turk Broda and Nick Metz made immediate waves when they joined the team and went on to contribute to its success into the '40s. But one of the biggest reasons for the Leafs' turnaround during the 1940s has to have been the change of coach from Dick Irvin to Clarence "Hap" Day.

Day made a name for himself in Toronto as a defenceman for the team from 1925 to 1937, and was loved by players and fans alike. Most importantly, Conn Smythe thought Day could motivate the Leafs in the playoffs after almost a decade of disappointment.

Day started his career with the Toronto St. Patricks as a forward, scoring 35 goals in 106 games, but when the team was sold to Conn Smythe, Day was moved to defence. That switch to the blue line shaped his view of hockey and also how he coached when he started working behind the bench for the Leafs.

Day's defensive system wasn't the most entertaining style of hockey for the fans, but it did prove effective. Day helped mould solid, defensive-minded players like Bob Davidson, Nick Metz and most importantly, goaltender Walter "Turk" Broda. Day elaborated on his defensive theories in an interview with Jack Batten in the book *The Leafs:* "Coaching offensively is too hard. You can give them a plan of attack, and then the situation for the plan may never come up in the game. But defence, now, think of all six men on the ice doing the job on defence. I told my players if they worked as hard coming back as they did going down the ice, we'd be okay. Of course, you had to have the proper type of player to handle that approach—or make them into the proper type."

By the end of the 1940–41 regular season, Day's system proved effective. The Leafs finished just a few points behind the Boston Bruins and looked primed to go far into the playoffs. Toronto was the only team that year to let in fewer than 100 goals. In 48 games, Turk Broda only allowed 99 goals for the best goals-against average in the league, good enough for his first Vezina Trophy.

The Maple Leafs would need every bit of defensive help they could get going up against the high-scoring Boston Bruins in the opening round of the 1941 playoffs. Boston had a formidable lineup with players such as Woody Dumart, Milt Schmidt, Bobby Bauer and "Mr. Zero" goaltender Frank Brimsek. The Leafs knew they would have to play their best if they were going to succeed against such a skilled team. It wasn't a bad outing for rookie coach Hap Day and his players as they matched the Bruins with some outstanding goaltending from Turk Broda and defence that kept Boston off the scoreboard. Despite predictions by sportswriters that the Bruins would take the series easily, the Maple Leafs managed to stretch it through seven games only to lose 2–1 in the final matchup. All was not lost for the Leafs. They had a solid team with a system that fit each player well and a goaltender they knew could perform under pressure in the playoffs. The experience gained from the 1941 opening-round loss to the Bruins would serve them well in the 1942 playoffs as the Leafs made one of the most exciting runs for the Stanley Cup in hockey history.

Few changes were made to the Maple Leafs lineup for the 1941–42 season and things continued with the same pace as the previous year. Toronto finished strong in second place behind the New York Rangers. Gordie Drillion and Syl Apps were the two standout Leafs players during the season, both ending up with 41 points. The two top teams would face off against each other in the opening round of the playoffs. Sports pundits heavily favoured the New York Rangers, given their outstanding season and offensive fire power thanks to scoring leaders Bryan Hextall, Lynn Patrick and Phil Watson. The Rangers knew Toronto would not be an easy team to beat, but they were confident they could finish the series off in six games or less.

In the first game of the series, Toronto surprised everyone except themselves with a 3–1 victory at home. The Rangers' top scorers were held off while the Leafs' top line of Apps, Drillion and Metz each contributed a goal. It was the same story in the second game as the Rangers could not muster any offence against the Leafs and the game ended with Toronto taking a commanding lead in the series after the 4–2 victory. The Rangers made the series a little more interesting with a decisive 3–0 shutout victory in game three, but the Leafs had the momentum and finished the Rangers off in six games. Meanwhile, the Detroit Red Wings had worked their way through the awful Montréal Canadiens and the Boston Bruins to make it into the Stanley Cup finals.

The Leafs weren't all that disappointed to get the Detroit Red Wings as opponents in the Cup finals. The Red Wings had finished the regular season with a mediocre record of 19–25–4 and were a little worn out from two physical series against the Canadiens and the Bruins. Detroit had a decent forward line with reliable goal scorers and set-up men such as Sid Abel, Don Grosso and Syd Howe, but their defencemen and their goaltender Johnny Mowers had struggled all season, making the Wings the favourites to bow out of the finals quickly. The local gambling establishments, aware of the Red Wings' shortcomings, had the Leafs as 8–5 favourites to win the Cup. Although he was keenly aware of his team's problems, Detroit coach Jack Adams said his Red Wings had one thing the Maple Leafs lacked.

"We may not have the greatest hockey club in the world, but it's a club that's loaded with fighting heart," Adams proudly exclaimed before his team faced the Leafs. "If there's anything that wins hockey championships, it's just that."

Longtime Toronto fans who remembered the days when Adams played for the Toronto Arenas and St. Patricks knew that if there was one coach out there who could instill a fighting spirit into a group of players, it was Adams. He was a loud, confrontational coach who was not afraid to berate a referee for a bad call or let a player know when he wasn't up to par. Adams would need this spirit and every trick in his book if he was to beat the Leafs in the finals.

In the first game, the Red Wings used every last bit of their fighting hearts to pound the Leafs into submission. Adams knew the Leafs played a tight, defensive game and that the only way to get to them was to hit them hard, fight for the puck in the corners and hope for a couple of lucky bounces.

Just two minutes into the game, Detroit's best forward during the regular season, Don Grosso, put his team on the scoreboard with a nice shot past Broda. The Leafs were obviously rattled by the Red Wings' constant pressure whenever they had the puck, and Toronto could not mount any significant offence. Luckily, the Leafs were able to put in two goals to make the game interesting for the fans, but a later goal by Grosso put the game out of reach for the Leafs. When the final buzzer sounded, the Red Wings had come away with a 3–2 victory. It would have been a greater goal difference had it not been for the stellar play of Leafs goaltender Turk Broda. The Leafs were at a loss to explain their inability to get any offence going against the Wings.

In the quiet Leafs dressing room after the game, coach Hap Day tried to explain to reporters what went wrong. "There's nothing wrong with our club physically. It's a question whether or not we've got the stuff that champions are made of. That wasn't hockey out there—it was a fair display of hoodlumism, Detroit's stock in trade! But we've got to adjust ourselves to the Kitty-bar-the-door tactics if we're going to win the Cup."

Detroit was full of confidence after game one. Everyone had predicted they would not last against the more powerful Leafs, but the Wings had proven they could compete—and maybe actually win the Cup in the process. Predictions still favoured Toronto despite the first loss, but after game two, the sportswriters would change their tune.

During the second game, Detroit kept up its system of dumping the puck into the Leafs' zone and forechecking heavily. The Red Wings were applying a simple philosophy, but the Leafs could not seem to figure a way around. Toronto had the most trouble with the line of Don Grosso, Eddie Wares and Sid Abel. Every time they stepped onto the ice, the Leafs looked tired and unprepared for the level of energy the trio brought to the game. Grosso was once again the star of the game, potting 2 goals and leading his team through another one-sided 4–2 victory.

"We out-fought them, out-hustled them and should have beat them 7–3," coach Jack Adams declared.

Detroit's simple system was working almost too well against the Leafs, and the players were overflowing with confidence before the start of the third game. "Those Leafs will know they've had their hides blistered when they get through this series," said Wings forward Sid Abel confidently.

Game three. Its importance was not lost on any of the Leafs players in the dressing room before the match. No team in the history of the National Hockey League had come back from a three-game deficit in the playoffs since the league instated the best-of-seven game format. There was a quiet tension among the players as they heard the crowds filing into Detroit's Olympia Arena, knowing it was not going to be easy to beat the Wings before a home crowd. Hap Day said what he could to put his players' minds at ease before they took to the ice, but he knew that the outcome of the game was completely up to them and how they played the next 60 minutes.

The Leafs silenced the noisy Detroit crowd with two quick goals in the first period from Lorne Carr, but the celebrations on the Leafs bench did not last long as the Detroit players answered with two of their own. In the second and third periods, the Red Wings increased their forechecking pressure, giving Toronto no room on the ice to get any offence started. By the final buzzer, the Red Wings scored five while Toronto had only managed the 2 goals from the first period.

"Detroit is unbeatable," said Toronto goaltender Turk Broda. "They're too hot and they can't seem to do anything wrong."

Day knew something had to change if the Leafs were going to pull through the series and win the Stanley Cup. He knew Detroit's system well enough, having played against them during the regular season, and knew the only way to beat them was to play their brand of dump'n'chase hockey. But Conn Smythe thought that playing style was amateurish and had forbidden Day from implementing that system with his Leafs.

"Smythe didn't like any system that involved giving the puck away," was how Day put it. But now that the Maple Leafs were on the verge of losing the Cup, Smythe retracted his objections to that style and allowed Day to make the necessary changes.

Day's first order of business in getting his team back on track was to bring in fresh legs to replace tired, injured veteran ones. Day decided to bench Bucko McDonald and Gord Drillion, who were not having a great series, and replace them with youngsters Bob Goldham and Don Metz. Day also introduced a new technique to combat Detroit's tough forechecking. In the first three games, Detroit had dominated by dumping the puck into the Leafs' zone, forechecking heavily and capitalizing on turnovers and lucky bounces. Day's answer was to do the same thing to Detroit. As soon as the puck was dumped into the Leafs' zone, they planned to simply dump it back out and forecheck the Wings in their zone.

Before the start of a game, a coach will usually try to inspire his team with a few wise words, but since that had not worked so far in the series, Day decided his players needed something different for inspiration. With minutes remaining before the opening faceoff, Day stood in the middle of the dressing room and summoned his players' attention. In his hands, he held a letter from a 14-year-old girl. She expressed her sadness that her Leafs could not beat the Red Wings and described how much it would hurt her if the Leafs could not win any games. Day folded up the letter, put it back in his pocket, and left the room. The players knew what they had to do.

"I remember sitting in that dressing room, waiting for the fourth game to start," said Syl Apps in an interview in Jack Batten's book *The Leafs*. "The only thing on our minds was, 'We can't go back to Toronto if we lose this game, too.' We were thinking we couldn't lose four straight and face the people back home."

Through the first few minutes of the game, Toronto was holding the Red Wings at bay, and Broda kept the Leafs in the game with some great saves. Yet despite all the changes and the hard work, the Leafs found themselves behind by 2 goals at the midway point of the second period. Although they were able to contain the Red Wings' most dangerous line of Grosso, Abel and Wares, Mud Bruneteau and Carl Liscombe were able to put the 2 goals by Broda. However, the Maple Leafs were not going to go down without a fight. By the end of the second period, they answered with 2 goals of their own and brought life back to the Leafs bench.

The Red Wings came back early in the third period to take the lead, but the Leafs knew that they could come back and did not panic. Two goals from Toronto's Syl Apps and Nick Metz put the Leafs ahead 4–3. Now all they had to do was to hold on to the lead. As if the close score were not enough entertainment for the fans, during a pause in play with just two minutes remaining in the game, Red Wing Eddie Wares directed a volley of verbal abuse at referee Mel Harwood. Wares was fuming over the referee's perceived bias against the Wings and the amount of penalties his team received. When Wares refused to leave the ice and continued his verbal assault, referee Harwood gave him a 10-minute misconduct. Moments after play resumed, Harwood spotted Detroit with too many men on the ice and whistled the play dead. Grosso was called out to serve the two-minute penalty, but he refused to go to the box without letting the referee know how displeased he was with the call. He increased his time in the box when he threw down his stick and gloves in front of the referee and offered to trade punches. Grosso finally took his place in the box and the game was allowed to continue. The game finished in relative calm, still 4–3 in favour of the Leafs, but when the final buzzer sounded all hell broke loose.

As Harwood worked out the final penalty count with the other off-ice officials, Detroit coach Jack Adams, still fuming over the penalties given out at the end of game, jumped onto the ice and headed straight for Harwood. Adams pounced on the unsuspecting referee and started throwing punches. While Harwood and the portly Adams traded haymakers in the penalty box, Detroit fans followed the coach's lead and began to attack the linesmen. The mob nearly got to league president Frank Calder, but police officers whisked him away before the crowd had a chance to vent its anger. When the dust settled and cooler heads prevailed, Adams was given a fine and suspended indefinitely. Living up to his reputation, he refused go without a fight.

"They can't keep me out of Maple Leaf Gardens. I'll buy my way into the place!" Adams said defiantly.

Those few remaining minutes in game four proved to be the turning point in the series. Before a packed crowd of over 15,000 fans at Maple Leaf Gardens, Toronto completely dominated the fifth game. The Red Wings found themselves in constant penalty trouble and the Leafs capitalized on every chance, ending the game with a 9–3 victory. Don Metz was the standout player for the Leafs with a hat trick, while the Red Wings' top line of Grosso, Wares and Abel was held off the scoresheet.

All the players were well-behaved for game six in Detroit. Toronto was now in complete control of the series, dominating every part of the game. Turk Broda was incredible in nets, helping his team to a 3–0 shutout. The changes made by Day seemed to be paying off, and the Leafs had the momentum going into the seventh and final Stanley Cup game at Maple Leaf Gardens.

When they had been down 3–0 in the series, fans and sports pundits had all but written the Maple Leafs off. Some 16,000 fans were back on the bandwagon and packed into Maple Leaf Gardens to see if their team could pull off one of the greatest miracles in National Hockey League history. The first whistle could barely be heard over the roar of the crowd as the referee signaled the starting lineups to take their places at centre ice. The noise from the crowd quickly fell off as Detroit scored the first goal of the game at just 1:44 of the first period. The Maple Leaf Gardens crowd members were on the edge of their seats as the second period went by and still the Leafs had not put in an equalizing goal.

Leafs fans across the hockey world breathed a collective sigh of relief when Sweeney Schriner tipped in a shot from the point to tie the game in the third period. The goal from Schriner seemed to send a message to the other Leafs, who suddenly took complete control of the game. Detroit coach Adams, who had managed to retake his place behind the bench for the final two games, paced nervously as he watched the Cup slowly disappear from his grasp. He tried different line combinations, shorter shifts and even yelling, but nothing could stop the Toronto's attack. The roof almost lifted off Maple Leaf Gardens when Pete Langelle put in the go-ahead goal in a mad scramble in front of the Red Wings net. Toronto sealed Detroit's fate when Schriner got the insurance goal late in the third period. The Leafs put up a wall of defence, giving the Red Wings no room to get any offence started. Adams could do nothing but watch as the seconds ticked off the clock. When the final buzzer sounded, the Maple Leafs poured onto the ice in celebration.

After the game, Jack Adams bitterly accepted his fate when confronted by the media. "Hap did a great job. Toronto deserved to win, I guess. But I think they were a little bit lucky," he added smugly.

The two weary teams lined up to shake hands after a hard-fought, entertaining series. Both teams were left with an equal amount of cuts, bruises and tired bodies, but only the Toronto Maple Leafs had the right to hold Lord Stanley's

Cup high above their heads in victory. The Leafs went down in the history of the National Hockey League as the only team ever to come back from a 3–0 deficit in the Stanley Cup final. (Since then, the only other team to come back from a 3–0 deficit in the playoffs was the 1975 New York Islanders against the Pittsburgh Penguins in the quarterfinals.)

Chapter Six

The Greatest Decade Continues

After their Cup win in 1942, the Toronto Maple Leafs underwent a major change in personnel. As World War II raged in Europe, the need for soldiers did not bypass the National Hockey League, and some of Toronto's best were called to duty. Along with owner Conn Smythe, the Maple Leafs lost the talents of Turk Broda, Syl Apps and Wally Stanowski. By the start of the 1944–45 season, of the 18 players who were on the roster for the 1942 Stanley Cup championship, only six remained. Filling in the ranks were a bunch of young kids called up from the minors and a group of aging veterans with the responsibility of keeping the Leafs at the top of the league. But while they had decent regular seasons between 1942 and 1944, the Leafs never really challenged for the top spot and made early exits from the playoffs at the hands of Detroit and Montréal.

With Conn Smythe in Europe, business manager Frank Selke, who was put in charge of the team's daily operations, saw his opportunity to make a few changes to the lineup to secure the future success of the Leafs. Smythe had always been quite particular when it came to moving certain players around, and Selke had trouble taking the steps he thought necessary to get quality players. One of the players for whom Smythe had a particular affinity was young defenceman Frankie Eddolls. Despite Smythe's warnings of swift retribution for trading players without his consent, Selke could not pass up an opportunity to make a deal for a young centre named Ted Kennedy.

Under contract with the Montréal Canadiens in 1942, Ted Kennedy moved from his hometown of Port Colborne, Ontario, at the tender age of 16 to Montréal to receive his training with the Montréal Royals. Feeling extremely homesick, the young Kennedy left Montréal and returned home to Ontario.

"I didn't like the environment. I just told them I was going back home," said Kennedy, looking back years later.

Back in Port Colborne, Kennedy continued to play for the local senior team under the coaching of hockey legend Nels Stewart. It was Stewart who recognized the natural talent the young Kennedy possessed and who told Selke he might be a good addition to the Leafs organization. Selke agreed and arranged a deal without Smythe's knowledge, swapping Montréal's rights to Kennedy for Frankie Eddolls. Smythe never forgave Selke for the trade, and Smythe's pride was hurt even more when Kennedy turned out to be one of the greatest players in Maple Leafs history. Things would only get worse between the two executives once Smythe returned from World War II in 1945.

While the boss was overseas, Selke had opened up the Maple Leaf Gardens to entertainment and rental opportunities, something Smythe had always been against. This large new source of revenue pleased the Gardens' board of directors, who wanted to remove Smythe from his dictatorial role in the organization and hand more power to Selke. Smythe was forced to fight to keep control of the team and the Gardens. In the end, Smythe won the battle for control but lost a valuable business partner and an astute hockey mind in Selke, who resigned in the summer of 1946 and joined the rival Montréal Canadiens organization. Years later, both men continued to argue over the reasons for their split.

"I think he respected my worth as a hockey manager but he could never admit that my ability for identifying hockey talent and moulding a team were far ahead of his," Selke said years later of the whole affair.

"Frank Selke always said for public consumption that he and I parted company because of a trade he made without my permission, while I was overseas. This is not true but probably sounds better, which is why Selke would say it," Smythe retorted.

With Kennedy a full contributing member of the team by the 1944–45 season, the Leafs were able to finish with a decent record but significantly behind the number one Montréal Canadiens. With Maurice "the Rocket" Richard, Elmer Lach and Toe Blake all leading the league in scoring, the Canadiens were the hands-down best team in the league that season. Richard had scored an incredible 50 goals in 50 games and goaltender Bill Durnan's low goals-against average made it difficult for opponents to win any games. The Canadiens had proven in the playoffs a year earlier that they had the best team when they marched over the Leafs in the first round and breezed by the Chicago Blackhawks in the finals in four straight games to win the Stanley Cup. They returned the next season with the same success during the regular season, and were the favourites to repeat as champions in the 1945 playoff run. But the Toronto Maple Leafs had other plans.

After the departure of Turk Broda, the Leafs signed Paul Bibeault as their number one goaltender, but he had a poor performance in the 1944 playoffs against the Canadiens (in the final game of that series, Bibeault let in 11 goals, 5 in the space of 3 minutes and 36 seconds). His replacement for the 1944–45 season was a goaltender by the name of Frank McCool, who wasn't anything like his name would lead you to believe. He was often so nervous before, after and during games that he had to drink milk to calm his ulcers.

With a team of unproven players and a goaltender prone to fits of anxiety, the Leafs were in tough in the first round of the 1945 playoffs against the Canadiens' powerful offence. McCool seemed up to the task in game one, and the Leafs' defence was able to shut out the Canadiens and win by the slimmest margin when Ted Kennedy scored with only 22 seconds remaining in the third period.

The physical intensity increased during game two, a close, checking affair. Frank McCool once again proved why he was named rookie of the year that season, stopping the Canadiens cold on many rushes. Montréal had to rely on its second and third lines as the Leafs completely eliminated the effectiveness of the "Punch Line," Richard, Lach and Blake. The bad blood boiled over into a few skirmishes, including a good punch-up between Montreal's Toe Blake and Toronto's Wally Stanowski.

Montréal won game three easily by a score of 4–1, showing the dominance that everyone expected. The Canadiens seemed on the verge of turning the series around in their favour at the start of game four with 2 goals from Lach and Richard, but the Leafs battled back to force the Canadiens into overtime. Twelve minutes into the first overtime period, after a faceoff to the right of Canadiens goaltender Durnan, Gus Bodnar snapped a quick shot past Durnan's right pad for the game-winning goal, putting a stranglehold on the series with the Leafs leading 3–1. Montréal came back in game five with an impressive 10–3 win, but Toronto had the Canadiens' number and knocked them out of the playoffs with a 3–2 win in game six.

In the Stanley Cup finals, the Toronto Maple Leafs were once again set to face Jack Adams and his Detroit Red Wings. The Leafs started off the series in excellent fashion with three straight victories to take a 3–0 grasp on the series. Frank McCool was outstanding in net for the Leafs through the first three games, not having let in one single goal. But the tide would soon turn in the Red Wings' favour.

Like the Leafs had done to them in the 1942 Stanley Cup final, the Red Wings mounted a miracle comeback. Detroit finally got through Frank McCool in game four, putting 5 goals past the Toronto goaltender. Ted Kennedy was the stand-out player for the Leafs during the game, scoring all 3 of Toronto's goals. Detroit goaltender Harry Lumley was the star player in game five, shutting out the Leafs 2–0 as the Red Wings jumped to 3–2 in the series. Both goaltenders were hot for the important game-six matchup in Toronto's Maple Leaf Gardens, shutting out the forwards on both teams up until the final buzzer. Eddie Bruneteau of the Detroit Red Wings ended the game at the 14-minute mark of the first overtime period.

Toronto now had to live with the possibility that the Red Wings could come back from a 3–0 deficit and do to the Leafs what they did to the Red Wings just three years earlier. Even with the Stanley Cup on the line, the Leafs were not worried about the outcome of the seventh game. "All we needed to be ready for the seventh game was a good night's sleep," said Leafs captain Bob Davidson years later. "We jumped on the train Saturday and went right to bed. I slept really good. So did the other guys. We were all feelin' okay by Sunday."

Feeling well rested and very confident, the Leafs came out strong in the first period of game seven and took the early lead when Ted Kennedy set up Mel Hill for a goal. Fans gathered at the Detroit Olympia Arena sat on the edge of their seats through the second period as their team came close to scoring but could not put one past McCool. Detroit fans breathed a sigh of relief when Murray Armstrong skated around Toronto's defence and fooled McCool for the equalizing goal. The game could now go either way. All one team needed was a lucky break, and at the halfway point of the third period, Toronto got that break when Detroit's Syd Howe cross-checked Gus Bodnar and got two minutes in the sin bin for his efforts. On the ensuing power play, Nick Metz carried the puck into the Detroit zone and shot it at Lumley. Lumley tried to smother it, but a collection of players swarming the net kept the puck bouncing dangerously in the crease. It bounced near Toronto's Babe Pratt, who took a couple of swings at the puck before eventually connecting and putting it past Lumley for the go-ahead goal. Frank McCool and the Toronto defence did the rest of the work, keeping the Red Wings at bay until the final buzzer sounded. Toronto had surprised everyone and won the Stanley Cup.

As Toronto celebrated its victory, the world could see that the war was slowly coming to an end, and players who had left years ago to defend their country slowly returned to their normal lives. Syl Apps, Don Metz, Bob Goldham and Billy Taylor all eventually made their way back to Maple Leaf Gardens, and hopes were high that with all the veteran players back on the ice, the Leafs would be a force to reckon with.

"There was a feeling among us, that, what with all the veterans returned, we were going to be home free in the league," said Syl Apps in Jack Batten's book *The Leafs*.

The only problem was that the Leafs could not translate that enthusiasm onto the ice. Frank McCool wanted too much money for Conn Smythe's liking, and the goalie refused to sign on for another season until the team brought in two second-string goaltenders. McCool eventually signed under the pressure of losing his job, but played like the two second-rate goalies. Even the return of Turk Broda could not bring any consistency between the Toronto pipes. Not one of the goaltenders finished with a winning record or anywhere near the top six in the league. To add to the problem, Ted Kennedy was out for the majority of the season with a severed tendon in his leg, and the Leafs were missing a major part of their offence. At the end of the 1945–46 season, the Leafs finished with an awful record of 19 wins, 24 losses and 7 ties and failed to make the playoffs.

They were obviously playing bad hockey, but there was a deeper reason for their fast downfall from Stanley Cup champions to the basement of the league. What the players failed to piece together until much later was that many of them had just come back from one of the most horrible events of the 20th century, and yet they had expected to just fall back into their regular lives. Most of the players had not put on skates for over two years, let alone picked up a stick. Once the players had more time to settle in, the Leafs went on one of the greatest Stanley Cup–winning streaks in NHL history to that date.

After a dismal season, Conn Smythe decided he would have to do something drastic to bring his team back into contention. Smythe thought the team needed some new talent and that the only way to accomplish this was to get rid of the older players. On their way out were veterans Sweeney Schriner, Frank McCool, Lorne Carr,

Babe Pratt and Billy Taylor. The rookies to join the club were forwards Howie Meeker, Vic Lynn and Joe Klukay and defencemen Garth Boesch, Jim Thomson, Gus Mortson and 20-year-old Bill Barilko. But the Leafs coach was not worried about the number of rookies on his starting lineup at the beginning of the 1946–47 season.

"Some of these men weren't real rookies," Day recounted in his later years. "Boesch, Meeker and some others – they'd matured in the army. I knew they'd measure up. They'd been through real battles."

Hap Day's normally defensive team suddenly became the top scorers in the NHL for the 1946–47 season. Almost every player contributed to the goal scoring that year (209 in total), and Turk Broda was once again solid in net, helping the Toronto Maple Leafs finish just a few points behind the defending Stanley Cup champion Montréal Canadiens. Defence was a little on the weaker side as the team had to rely mostly on the inexperienced players, but it was the playoffs where the rookies needed to prove themselves— and that's exactly what they did.

Ted Kennedy led the way for his Leafs against the Detroit Red Wings in the first round of the playoffs. The Leafs won every game of the series except a 9–1 anomaly in game two. Detroit was not yet the dominant team that they would become in the 1950s, and the Leafs easily took them out in five games. The Montréal Canadiens had a more difficult time with the Boston Bruins, but still managed to eliminate them in five games. This set up a meeting between old rivals.

For the first time since their dispute, former Leafs coach Dick Irvin and former Leafs business manager Frank Selke, now with the Canadiens, met again, this time in the Stanley Cup finals. A lot of pride was on the line in this highly anticipated series.

Sports pundits did not give any predictions as to which team would take the series, given that they both were pretty evenly matched. But after game one, when the Canadiens massacred the Leafs in a 6–0 shutout, many fans began to see the writing on the wall that the Leafs were simply outmatched. "How did these guys get into the playoffs?" asked Canadiens goaltender Bill Durnan in a post-game scrum with the media.

Durnan would eat his words just two days later, when the Leafs returned the favour with a 4–0 shutout in game two. The Canadiens also lost their star player, Maurice "the Rocket" Richard, after he lost his temper and slashed two Leafs players over the head before being given a match penalty and a one-game suspension. Back in

Toronto without their star player, the Canadiens dropped game three to the Leafs by a score of 4–2. Toronto kept up the momentum in game four, taking a 3–1 lead in the series after a long, tough battle that needed 16 minutes of overtime before captain Syl Apps scored the winner. The Canadiens came back with a 3–1 victory in Montréal for game five, but the Leafs' young defencemen shut down the Habs' offence in game six and took the game by a slim margin of 2–1. The gamble Smythe had taken on the rookie line-up paid off with a great, energetic team and the Maple Leafs' third Stanley Cup of the decade.

The next year, the Leafs dominated the regular season as their old rivals the Montréal Canadiens struggled after losing the services of Toe Blake, who suffered a career-ending ankle fracture. That didn't mean the Leafs were left without any competition. The Detroit Red Wings had a few rookies of their own, and one in particular was quickly making a name for himself in the league. Gordie Howe already had one season under his belt at the start of the 1947–48 season and was just coming into his own as one of the premier power forwards in the league. Despite this grow-ing talent in Detroit, the Leafs were still the champions.

Toronto opened the regular season with six straight victories, but after the Leafs lost one game, Conn Smythe thought he needed to make a change and backed up his team's scoring power with one of the biggest trades in National Hockey League history. Smythe sent Gaye Stewart, Gus Bodnar, Bud Poile, Bob Goldham and Ernie Dickens to the Chicago Blackhawks for scoring all-star Max Bentley and rookie Cy Thomas. With Bentley leading the Leafs' scoring sheet, Toronto finished off the season with a record of 32–15–13. The Red Wings finished just a few points behind the Leafs, setting up what many thought would be the two teams challenging each other in the finals.

As expected, it was the Toronto Maple Leafs against the Detroit Red Wings in the Stanley Cup final. But it wasn't the exciting offensive hockey extravaganza that many people anticipated from the two top teams. Toronto was never challenged by the Red Wings, who never scored more than 3 goals on Turk Broda and lost the final game by a score of 7–2. Toronto swept the Red Wings in four games straight to win their second consecutive Stanley Cup.

As Cup champions for the two straight seasons, many expected the Leafs to have another successful year in 1948–49. But a collection of injuries and a few heads grown big from success led the Leafs down the losing path that season. With a few games remaining in the regular season, they were even on the cusp of not making it into the playoffs, but a last-minute run of victories pushed them over the edge and into the first round of the post-season.

While the Leafs struggled all season to win games, as soon as they hit the post-season, they began to show the form that had won them two consecutive Stanley Cups. The Boston Bruins finished second overall in the league and were the favourites to beat Toronto, but after a 3–0 shellacking in the first game at the hands of the Leafs, the Bruins were never able to make a dent in the series. Despite one overtime win in game three, the Bruins could not mount any significant opposition to the Leafs and were eliminated in five games. Meanwhile, the Detroit Red Wings were embroiled in a tense battle with the Montréal Canadiens. The series was a showdown between the two top goaltenders in the regular season, Bill Durnan (number one) against the Red Wings' Harry Lumley (number two). Both goalies were at the top of their game for the series, keeping the scores low and the fans on the edge of the seats. The series needed seven games before the Red Wings would emerge the victors.

The Leafs, who had finished their series against the Bruins on March 30, got a much-appreciated break, starting the Stanley Cup finals against the Red Wings on April 8. The Red Wings got only three days' rest after a tough seven-game series against the Habs.

The Red Wings were just too exhausted to mount any kind of resistance against the well-rested Leafs. After winning game one in overtime on a Joe Klukay goal, the Maple Leafs never looked back and took out the Red Wings again in four straight games. Toronto's defensive lines did a fantastic job of shutting down Detroit's top line of Sid Abel, Gordie Howe and Ted Lindsay, and Turk Broda never let in more than 2 goals in one game throughout the short series. Toronto had the first Stanley Cup "three-peat" in National Hockey League history and would have one more moment of glory in the early 1950s before fading out of contention for a decade.

Chapter Seven

1951

The top-10 NHL scoring leaders by the end of the 1950–51 season were made up mostly of players from the Detroit Red Wings and the Toronto Maple Leafs. The Red Wings definitely had the more potent offence, but the Maple Leafs were no slouches either. Once again, Conn Smythe made a few changes to the lineup that proved helpful to the team in the goal-scoring department. Bill Ezinicki and Vic Lynn were traded off to the Boston Bruins and a youngster named Tod Sloan was called in to take up an important position beside Ted Kennedy and Sid Smith. Smythe realized that the recent increase in the amount of games played during the season was starting to wear down veteran goaltender Turk Broda, so he brought in rookie Al Rollins to help share the burden in goal. Smythe also decided that Hap Day's time behind the bench as coach of the Toronto Maple Leafs had come to an end. Day was moved into the assistant general manager's office, and former player "Gentleman" Joe Primeau was named the new head coach. Smythe's subtle changes made a great difference in the team's success as the Leafs remained hot on Detroit's heels the entire regular season in the fight for first place overall.

Toronto finished just six points behind the Red Wings at the end of the season with 95 points, and their two-goaltender combination finished with the best goals-against average in the league. Al Rollins took home the Vezina Trophy for his efforts in goal for the Maple Leafs. When the post-season finally got under way, the Leafs were set to play the Boston Bruins and the Red Wings took on the Montréal Canadiens in the other playoff series. Everyone expected that the Stanley Cup final would be a showdown between the two top teams, given that they had both finished more than 30 points ahead of the third- and fourth-place teams.

Toronto lost the first game against the Bruins 2–0 but bounced back as expected and won the next four games to move into the Stanley Cup finals for the sixth time in the last decade. In the other series, the Detroit Red Wings had their hands full with the Montréal Canadiens. The first two games went into quadruple and triple overtime, respectively, with the Canadiens winning both games. Although the Red Wings won two games, the Canadiens were too strong and upset the Wings in six games, setting up a meeting between two of the biggest rivals in sports history. Toronto had the advantage in this matchup, having finished ahead of the Canadiens during the regular season, but Montréal was riding high after eliminating the top team in the league and wasn't about to go quietly into the night. The stage was set for one of the most unique and dramatic finals in the history of the Stanley Cup.

Toronto and Montréal had already firmly established a rivalry through decades of battling for hockey supremacy in Canada. This series would elevate the rivalry to new heights and make a legend out of one player in particular.

Game one of the series got under way in Toronto and things started off well for the Maple Leafs when just 15 seconds into the first period, Sid Smith scored, causing Maple Leaf Gardens to explode in a deafening roar from the capacity crowd. Toronto and Montréal traded a few goals and when the final buzzer sounded the score was tied at two, requiring overtime to resolve the first game of the series. Montréal's Gerry McNeil and Toronto's Turk Broda seemed up to the task, turning away some difficult shots in the early stages of overtime. But it was once again Toronto's Sid Smith who made the difference, scoring his second goal of the game at 5:51 of extra time on a beautiful backhand that fooled McNeil. Toronto was excited after winning the game but also a little tired after the physically draining contest and the extra time spent on the ice during overtime. Overtime was something both teams were going to have to get used to in this series.

The second game was just as entertaining for the capacity crowd at Maple Leaf Gardens. It was another tight, high-pressure, hard-hitting affair that either team could win down to the last minutes. The Canadiens got on the board first with a goal from Paul Masnick and then got an insurance goal when Billy Reay put the Habs ahead by two on a setup from Maurice Richard. Usually, when the home team goes down by 2 goals, the fans tend to get quieter as the game slowly ticks by, but Maple Leafs fans never gave up hope that their team would come back and were eventually rewarded with late goals in the second and third periods to send the game yet again into overtime. But this time, the thousands of Toronto fans would be disappointed. Montréal got the first few good chances and clinched it when defenceman Doug Harvey coolly made his way through centre ice and shot a pass to Maurice

Richard, who had snuck in behind the defence. Turk Broda left his crease to cut down the angle as Richard wound up for the blast, but the Rocket found a hole and put the puck behind Broda for the game-winning goal. With the series tied, the two teams packed up their bags and headed to La Belle Province for the next two games.

Even though Turk Broda was playing at the top of his game, Toronto coach Joe Primeau was a little worried that the portly veteran's body could not take much more abuse and decided to go with Al Rollins for the remainder of the series. It didn't appear to be such a good decision when Maurice Richard shot in a juicy rebound off Rollins' leg pad after just 2:18 had passed in the first period of game three. Primeau did not waver in his belief that Rollins was the right man for the job, however, and his trust in the rookie goaltender paid off. Rollins shut the door to the Canadiens snipers for the rest of the game while his teammates helped him out and tied the game before the end of the third period for yet another overtime nail-biter. Less than five minutes had passed in the first overtime period when Ted Kennedy blasted a bad-angled shot past a surprised Gerry McNeil for the winning goal, giving Toronto a 2–1 series lead.

The fourth game was almost a carbon copy of the first, with Toronto's Sid Smith and Montréal's Maurice Richard breaking the ice for their teams. The rivals once again could not solve their differences in the allotted 60 minutes of play and required another overtime period to declare a winner. Toronto knew that Montréal relied too much on Maurice Richard for their goal production and that by keeping him away from the net, they had a better chance of taking the game. The new strategy proved effective, and it gave the Leafs' Harry Watson enough time to put the game-winning goal past McNeil for the 3–1 series lead. The teams headed back to Maple Leaf Gardens for game five.

Toronto had the advantage going into game five, but they were not taking the Canadiens for granted. Montréal had a fast team, and Maurice Richard was a constant threat on the ice. The Canadiens would have to count on hard work and a little luck to get back into the series. It was do or die time for Montréal.

Gerry McNeil was outstanding behind the Canadiens net, keeping his team alive with save after save until Rocket Richard took some pressure off when he scored a highlight-reel goal while carrying Toronto defenceman Jim Thomson on his back. The Canadiens attempted to stem the Leafs' attack with some heavy physical play, but they still could not stop the Leafs from tying up the game. The Habs seemed to have the wind knocked out of them when Canadiens forward Bob Dawes missed a check on Ted Kennedy and suffered a compound fracture to his right leg. Despite losing a player, Montréal somehow managed to score the go-ahead goal and carried that lead well into the third period. But with less than one minute left, Joe Primeau decided to pull Rollins in favour of an extra attacker, praying that the Leafs would tie the game to force overtime once again. Montréal tried to throw up a defensive wall, but the Leafs were able to get the puck and carry it into the Canadiens' zone. The Leafs' Max Bentley had a little time to survey the ice, and spotted Tod Sloan and Sid Smith posted to the left and right of goaltender Gerry McNeil. The Canadiens' big defenceman Butch Bouchard rushed Bentley to poke the puck away from him, but Bentley managed to get a pass off toward Smith. With no pressure from any Canadiens defencemen and goaltender Gerry McNeil caught out of position, Smith passed the puck across the goal crease to Tod Sloan who simply redirected the puck into the wide-open net.

"The fans hollered so much I think the noise lasted 15 minutes. I never heard anything like it," said Max Bentley years later. "It seemed like they must've kept up right through the intermission before the overtime, that loud, loud crowd noise."

Once again, overtime was necessary to end the game, but this time, with Toronto leading the series 3–1, it was a battle for hockey's ultimate prize. Montréal pressed hard in the first few moments of the period, but Toronto got the first scoring chance. Primeau went with the Gardner, Meeker and Watson line up front, backed by Boesch and Barilko on defence. At around the two-minute mark, Meeker carried the puck into the Canadiens zone and set himself up behind Montréal goaltender McNeil. Meeker was looking for the pass out front. Canadiens defenceman Tom Johnson rushed Meeker and forced him to make a pass out front to waiting Leafs player Harry Watson. Because the puck was bouncing on edge, Watson did not get off a good shot, and Gerry McNeil made the save by diving to the left corner of the net. The puck bounced off McNeil and ended up in front of the net. Spotting the loose puck, Toronto defenceman Bill Barilko, who was not known for his offensive talents, rushed in from the blue line, took one swipe at the puck and just beat McNeil as he tried to bat it out of the air. Maple Leaf Gardens exploded in a chorus of cheers for the new

Stanley Cup champions and the hero of the game, Bill Barilko. The Maple Leafs players rushed off the bench, hoisted the young defenceman on their shoulders and paraded him around the rink.

Coach Joe Primeau had told Barilko all year that the slap shot was just a hockey fad and that it would never become a useful tool in the NHL. But Barilko was the one who got the final word. "I told you it was a deadly shot," Barilko yelled to Primeau in the dressing room after the amazing game.

Conn Smythe admitted after the game that Barilko had been close to going back to the minors. "At times he was such a problem, I wanted to send him down to Pittsburgh, but thank God we kept him!" Smythe said.

After the celebrations began to calm down, Barilko and his friend Dr. Henry Hudson decided they needed to get out of the big city and fly up north for a week of fishing on Ontario's Seal River. After a short refueling stop for their small plane, the two friends took off for their final destination. But when they did not arrive or return from their fishing trip, a search-and-rescue team was immediately dispatched. People on the ground and in planes searched the dense forests of northern Ontario where the plane was last reported seen, but after weeks of exhaustive searching, the fate of the Maple Leafs defenceman and his friend remained a mystery. Over the years, several rumours circulated about the reason for Barilko's strange disappearance. One of the most ridiculous theories had Barilko defecting to the Soviet Union to teach young hockey players the Canadian style of game. It wasn't until 11 years later, in 1962, that the mystery of Bill Barilko's disappearance was finally solved. A plane passing over a remote section of forest near Cochrane, Ontario, spotted a piece of metal shining through the forest growth. When a team of investigators was sent in, they found the same small plane that Barilko and Hudson were last seen in and two skeletons still strapped in their seats.

Even stranger still was the fact that from the moment Barilko scored that winning goal in overtime, the Toronto Maple Leafs didn't win another Stanley Cup until the year his body was discovered. Because of his mysterious disappearance, the history attached to his overtime winner and the Leafs' 11-year Cup drought until his body was found, Barilko's story has leapt from the pages of history to the stuff of myth. Canadian band The Tragically Hip immortalized Barilko's story in their 1992 hit song "Fifty Mission Cap,"

bringing the young Leafs defenceman's story to
a whole new generation:

"Bill Barilko disappeared that summer,

he was on a fishing trip.

The last goal he ever scored

won the Leafs the Cup.

They didn't win another until 1962,

the year he was discovered.

I stole this from a hockey card,

I keep tucked up under

my fifty mission cap, I worked it in

to look like that."

Chapter Eight

The Fabulous '60s

After that 1951 Stanley Cup win, things started to go sour for the Toronto Maple Leafs. From 1951 to 1959, the Leafs never finished the regular season higher than third overall and only once made it to the Stanley Cup final, which they lost to the Canadiens in 1959. The team that had more than five players in the top-20 scoring leaders in 1950–51 had just two, Ted Kennedy and Sid Smith, by 1954–55. During that decade, the team that had prided itself in having one of the toughest defences in the league let in more goals than they scored for five seasons. Their worst season came in 1957–58, when they won 21 games, lost 38 and tied 11, finishing in last place for the first time in franchise history.

Yet things were not all doom and gloom for the Toronto team. Ted Kennedy kept up his stellar offensive play and leadership, taking home the Hart Trophy in 1954–55 as the league's most valuable player. Sid Smith was named to several all-star games and took home a couple of Lady Byng Trophies for his gentlemanly conduct on the ice.

In goal, things weren't so bad during the early part of the decade. With Turk Broda bowing out of the league after the Stanley Cup win in 1951, the task of guarding the Maple Leafs net was left in the very capable hands of Al Rollins. During the 1951–52 season, Rollins played all 70 games and finished just second in goals-against average behind Detroit's Terry Sawchuk. But Rollins' days with the Leafs were numbered, and during the summer of 1952 he was traded to the Chicago Blackhawks for goaltender Harry Lumley. In his second and third seasons with the Leafs, Lumley finished as the top goaltender in the league, taking home the Vezina Trophy for his efforts in 1954. Without Lumley in goal, the Leafs' numbers surely would have been much worse than they were.

As bad as things were getting on the ice, off the ice it was worse. Conn Smythe was spending more and more time away from Maple Leaf Gardens with his stable of racehorses. The rigors of professional hockey management were starting to wear on the aging Smythe, and slowly he started to cede power to those he trusted most. On February 1, 1955, Smythe stepped down as the Leafs general manager and gave Hap Day the responsibility of running his team's affairs. Smythe's son, Stafford, wanted to get his hands on Daddy's business and convinced his father to name him and a group of others to a hockey advisory committee. The idea was to let Stafford get a sense of how things worked so he could perhaps take over one day. Among the group hand-picked by Stafford was a young lawyer named Harold Ballard, who would later change the history of the Toronto Maple Leafs franchise. With the committee in place, the constant chorus of voices chiming in on every hockey decision left the Leafs management without clear direction. As a result, the team suffered.

Nowhere was this more evident than in the selection of head coaches. When Joe Primeau retired in 1953 to focus on his personal business affairs, the Leafs were left without a replacement. Looking through the team's past ranks, the hockey advisory committee thought it wise to appoint former Maple Leafs great King Clancy as head coach. Clancy did what he could with the Leafs from 1953 to 1956, but after Toronto fell to a record of 24–33–13, he was unceremoniously bounced from the job. Next up for the post was another former Maple Leafs great,

Howie Meeker. Everybody liked the decision to place Meeker behind the Toronto bench—everybody but Conn Smythe. "If he has a team of Rocket Richards and four more like him, he couldn't win," was how Smythe put it. Meeker gave the job his best shot, but after finishing the season 10 points out of last place, he was removed. Billy Reay was selected as the next coach, but he took the Leafs even lower, finishing with the worst record in the franchise's history.

The shakeups continued after the Leafs' worst season. Hap Day left his job as general manager and was—amazingly—replaced by failed coach Howie Meeker, who lasted only a few months before being fired. Stafford Smythe decided to leave the position empty during the 1957–58 season and finally found a replacement who would take the Leafs out of the basement of the league and bring back some respectability to Maple Leaf Gardens. The hiring of George "Punch" Imlach as general manager and head coach of the Leafs would turn Toronto's fortunes around and make it one of the best NHL teams of the 1960s.

Even though the Leafs were playing some of their worst hockey, they added several young players who would make the 1960s the decade of the Toronto Maple Leafs. Most notably among the team's new recruits were the tall, strapping forward Frank Mahovlich and the ageless goaltender Johnny Bower.

When Mahovlich joined the Maple Leafs, the team hoped that the six-foot-tall, 205-pound young man would help turn the fortunes of the team around. He was one of the lone bright spots in the team's worst year on record in 1957–58. Mahovlich was under constant pressure to perform and was often the target of media criticism, but one could not argue with the points. By 1960–61, Mahovlich led the Leafs in scoring with 48 goals and 36 assists and was an indispensable part of the Leafs' Stanley Cup success in the '60s.

The other major reason for the Maple Leafs' turnaround in the '60s was Johnny Bower's goaltending. Bower got his start in the National Hockey League with the New York Rangers in 1953–54, but he was shipped back to the minors after just one season. He eventually caught the eye of Leafs coach Billy Reay, who signed him to a two-year contract. In his first year with the Leafs, Bower helped them into the playoffs and all the way into the finals before the team lost to the Montréal Canadiens in five games. Bower was a true professional who played all of his angles well and perfected the fine art of the goal-tender poke check.

"I never enjoyed being scored on by anyone regardless of the situation. During practice it was all business for me. Because of my age, I was constantly working on my angles and I took a lot of pride in making saves against my teammates or any opponents," Bower said years later about his time as a Leaf.

Bower's actual age was always in question. He had a face that could have put him anywhere between 35 and 50, but he played like he was still in his 20s. In reality, he was 35 when he joined the Leafs and played with the club until he was an incredible 46 years old. He would remain the Leafs' number one goaltender through the 1960s and become one of the most loved players on the team.

After several years of poor hockey and bad management, Toronto Maple Leafs fans were finally rewarded with some entertaining hockey during the 1958–59 season. Still getting used to Punch Imlach's style of coaching, the Leafs were able to dig themselves out of the cellar of the league and put themselves into a playoff spot for the first time in two years. No one expected the Leafs to make any headway in the playoffs given their losing record of 27–32–11, but the one thing the Maple Leafs had been lacking for the majority of the '50s they now had in abundance: chemistry. The Leafs had all the ingredients of a winning team—Imlach just needed the entire season to work out the kinks. By the time the playoffs came around, though, most people had already written the Leafs off. But when they dispensed of the second-place Boston Bruins in seven games to move on against the powerful Canadiens, many critics had to re-evaluate their opinion. The pundits actually got it right in the Stanley Cup final when the Leafs faced off against the Stanley Cup champion Montréal Canadiens, who beat Toronto in five games. Even though they lost, the Leafs had made their mark.

The Maple Leafs gave their fans something to cheer about during the 1959–60 regular season when they finished with a winning record for the first time in five years. The Leafs were in second place behind the Montréal Canadiens and primed for a good playoff run. They beat up on the Red Wings in six, but their luck ran out when they ran up against the reigning Cup champs again. Montréal was simply too strong a team and easily took out the Leafs in four straight games. Soon, it would be Toronto's turn.

The Maple Leafs finished the 1960–61 season just two points behind the leading Montréal

Canadiens. But the two top teams would not advance into the finals this time, as it was the Chicago Blackhawks' year to shine. Toronto lost to Detroit in the semifinals in five games, and the Blackhawks went on to beat the Red Wings for the Stanley Cup.

The 1961–62 season began the decade of the Toronto Maple Leafs. Adding players like Red Kelly and Eddie Shack gave the Leafs the added leadership, scoring touch and pure personality needed to take the team to the next level. Only Frank Mahovlich, Red Kelly and George Armstrong were among the top-20 leaders in scoring during the regular season, but still the Leafs finished with 232 goals. All levels were now contributing, and the Leafs eased into the playoffs ready for what lay ahead. Exactly what was to come for the Toronto Maple Leafs was a semifinal battle with the New York Rangers.

It was a contentious battle from the first faceoff of the series at the Maple Leaf Gardens. To the delight of the Toronto faithful, their home team checked the Rangers into submission, winning the first two games of the series in a convincing fashion. It seemed home-ice advantage played a big role in the series as the New York Rangers satisfied their hometown fans' lust for victory with a narrow 5–4 win in game three and a more convincing effort of 4–2 in game four. When a series is tied 2–2, there is nothing more important for a team than to take game five and get the advantage for the final win. Many series have been won on the efforts of a team to go up 3–2 in a series, and with the Toronto Maple Leafs that year, it would be no different—but that didn't mean the Rangers were going to make life easy for them.

Johnny Bower put on a goaltending clinic for game five, keeping his team in the game and only allowing 2 goals. On the other end of the ice, Rangers goaltender Lorne "Gump" Worsley was having an even more difficult time as the Maple Leafs peppered him with shot after shot. As always, the diminutive goaltender was up to the task, and by the end of the third period, the score was tied at two. After the first overtime period, it was clear that the only way either team was going to win was with a little luck. Both goaltenders had seen too many pucks in their careers to let in a soft goal so late in an important game, and they were not about to start slipping in overtime of a Stanley Cup playoff.

After the end of the first overtime, both teams had had their chances, but the puck just wasn't falling where they wanted and the goaltenders weren't making things any easier. There were a few close calls, but nothing for the fans to cheer about. They had to wait till a few minutes into the second overtime before they got what they came for.

The Leafs carried the puck into the Rangers' zone. Mahovlich skated around, looking for a spot to get open for a pass. The moment he found enough real estate on the ice, the Toronto defence whipped him the puck, and Mahovlich immediately fired a shot on net. Worsley stopped the blast but lost sight of the puck. Doing what every good goalie should in such situations, Worsley immediately fell to the ice, hoping to cover the puck. The only problem was that Worsley couldn't see the puck because it lay just under his head. Red Kelly was hovering around the net, caught sight of the puck, and poked it in for the game-winning goal. As Maple Leaf Gardens exploded, Worsley shook his head in disbelief. Luck was on the Leafs' side this time.

The Leafs polished off the Rangers in the next game, knocking 7 goals by the broken Worsley to move onto the next round against Chicago. The Blackhawks had disposed of the Canadiens in a repeat performance of the previous year. Goalie Glenn Hall was once again the difference. The Canadiens could not figure him out.

The series against the Rangers showed that the Leafs were simply a better team all around and just needed a few extra games to prove it, but against the Chicago Blackhawks, they had a different set of problems that would call for some old Leafs strategies from Hap Day's playbook.

Chicago had an excellent goaltender in Glenn Hall and some of the finest defensive specialists in guys such as Dollard St-Laurent and Pierre Pilote. However, looking over their goal scorers, they had incredible point-scoring machines Bobby Hull and Stan Mikita, but not much else. The two players were in some way responsible for over 70 percent of the 217 goals scored by the Blackhawks during the regular season. Imlach was faced with the same problem Day had encountered when confronting the Montréal Canadiens, or more specifically, Maurice "the Rocket" Richard. Once again, the Leafs had to shut down the top goal producers. So the team decided to make it the specific job of several players to shadow Hull and Mikita so that neither of the two dangerous Hawks would be able to break loose for a goal. It turned out that the theory worked well when put into practice.

Imlach worked the defensive system to perfection in the first two games of the series held in Toronto, which the Leafs won by scores of 4–1 and 3–2. Chicago fought back to win game three in a convincing fashion, using the energy from their hometown fans to shut out the Leafs 3–0. The Blackhawks caught a lucky break in game four when Johnny Bower pulled a hamstring muscle in the first period and was forced to sit out the remainder of the playoffs. Into the Toronto goal went Don Simmons. He played only nine games during the regular season but had proven sharp in each start. Imlach had only one question left: could his backup goaltender come through under pressure? Imlach sweated out the rest of game four as Simmons let in several soft goals on the way to a 4–1 loss. The goalie redeemed himself in game five with a little help from his teammates in an 8–4 victory. The defence shut down the two powerful Black-hawks while the offence kicked into gear and exploded for a flurry of goals late in the game. That left just one more win to go for the Leafs to have their first Stanley Cup of the decade.

Game six. Hall and Simmons put on a goaltending exhibit, not allowing a single goal until late in the third period, when Bobby Hull broke the ice with a slap shot past Simmons. A few seconds later, the Leafs came right back on a goal from Bob Nevin to equal the score. Toronto put the game away when Tim Horton led a beautiful rush into the Hawks zone and drilled a pass to

Dick Duff, who blasted a one-timer past Glenn Hall for the game-winning goal. The Leafs put up the defensive barricade and the Hawks could not get through in the remaining minutes of the game. The Leafs won the Cup. As they celebrated their sweet victory that summer, they paused to remember a former teammate whose body was found 11 years after he disappeared.

For the 1962–63 season, the Leafs were at the top of their game, finishing the regular season in first place overall. The Leafs had a perfect balance of defence, offence and great goaltending, making them the toughest team to play that season. Toronto yet again proved themselves in the playoffs, shutting down the high-scoring, high-flying Montréal Canadiens in five games in the semifinals, moving on to the Detroit Red Wings for the Stanley Cup finals. Johnny Bower carried over his success in goal from the Montréal series and was stellar in net against the Red Wings. The Wings could not produce an offence against Toronto, while every Leafs line contributed. Detroit could not form any adequate resistance, and the Maple Leafs dispensed with them in five games to win their second consecutive Stanley Cup championship.

The 1963–64 version of the Toronto Maple Leafs returned with almost the same lineup but this season, they looked nothing like the champs that breezed their way past Montréal and Detroit. After a bumpy regular season that saw the departure of veterans Dick Duff and Bob Nevin, the Leafs managed to battle their way into third spot overall and a first-round playoff spot against perennial rivals the Montréal Canadiens. Duff and Nevin had been regular contributors on the scoresheet, but the 1963–64 season saw both their goal outputs drop to just seven apiece with only a few games remaining in the season. Imlach unloaded them on the New York Rangers in return for high-scoring forward Andy Bathgate and utility player Don McKenney.

Playoff time, and the Leafs showed the same difficulties they had during the regular season. Plagued by inconsistent play, they traded wins and losses with the Canadiens in the first-round semifinal, forcing a deciding game seven much to the displeasure of coach Punch Imlach. He knew he had a winning team, but the Leafs seemed to have lost the chemistry that brought them two previous Stanley Cups. Luckily for Imlach, he had Dave Keon on his side for game seven. Keon took the game into his hands and scored all three of the Leafs' goals. Toronto won the series 4–3 and moved on to the finals against the Detroit Red Wings. The Red Wings had fought a tough semifinal battle against the

Chicago Blackhawks and were just as tired and worn down as the Leafs. But the Red Wings wanted revenge for the previous Stanley Cup losses to the Leafs and were not about to hand the trophy over again.

Game one took place at Toronto's Maple Leaf Gardens, and much to the delight of local fans, the Leafs won the opening game of the series by a close margin of 3–2. Detroit came back with two wins to take a 2–1 series lead. Toronto was forced to battle back from behind each time and needed a desperate win in game six to keep alive their chances of three consecutive Cups.

Game six was the pivotal game of the series and one of the most memorable nights in Leafs history. The Red Wings were without a doubt the better team, but Johnny Bower was the difference for the Leafs, giving them the confidence on the back end so they could take a few chances up front. The Detroit team was leading 3–2 by the halfway point of the second period when Toronto's Billy Harris scored on Terry Sawchuk after receiving a pass from Dave Keon. Bower almost stood on his head making saves throughout the third period to keep the Leafs alive. The Leafs took a hit to their lineup when Gordie Howe crossed their blue line and blasted a low shot that found its way onto the small, unprotected area between the skate boot and the shin pad of tough Leafs defenceman Bob Baun.

"I heard a boom like a cannon," Baun said. "It was the bone cracking."

Like a true tough hockey player, Baun tried to stay in position to stop the Red Wings' advance, but the pain was just too much, and he collapsed to the ice. Baun had to be carried off on a stretcher and taken to the dressing room, where his leg was taped up and frozen. The team doctor wanted to have Baun transported for X-rays, but the defenceman refused, opting to return to play once the freezing killed the pain.

The third period continued with neither team able to break the tie. The final buzzer sounded and the two teams headed into overtime for the second time that series. Surprising everyone in the arena, Bob Baun took his place on the Leafs bench for the overtime period. Baun gave the thumbs-up to Imlach that he was okay to play and was sent out in the early moments of the overtime. Baun wasn't moving as well as usual, but he still managed to follow the play into the Detroit zone. Stationed at the point, Baun took a pass from George Armstrong and fired a shot at Terry Sawchuk. The Detroit goaltender would have had no problem stopping that shot on most occasions except that Baun's shot deflected off

Red Wings defenceman Bill Gadsby and bounced into the net. Baun had scored the game-winning goal in overtime on a broken leg, but still the tough defenceman was not finished. The Leafs managed to stay alive and force a deciding game seven at home in Toronto.

After the game, Baun was noticeably wincing as he limped around the dressing room. He refused the team doctor's advice to get an X-ray because he knew they would discover the broken bone and not allow him to play in the seventh game. So despite his injury, Baun suited up for the match and played all his regular shifts. The Leafs completely dominated the broken Wings and won the final game by a score of 4–0, taking home their third consecutive Stanley Cup victory.

As for Bob Baun, he finally did get that X-ray, which revealed a broken shinbone. Explaining his ability to play in two games despite the pain, Baun said, "I guess it was my pain tolerance and the mental ability to block things out." After the amazing story got out, the tougher coaches around the league were heard to say to their injured players, "If Baun can play on a broken leg, what's your excuse?"

Chapter Nine

The Fall of the Empire

The erosion of the foundation of the Leafs' empire probably began when Conn Smythe sold his controlling interest in the Maple Leaf Gardens in 1962 to his son, Stafford, and businessmen John Basset and Harold Ballard. Under the new management, Maple Leaf Gardens slowly lost its traditions to profits. More seats were added, ticket prices were raised, advertisements were added everywhere, and the famous bandstand was removed to make room for more seats. But it wasn't the changes to the building that would finally bring the team down, it was the changes going on in the front office.

While Stafford Smythe ran the hockey operations, Harold Ballard took control of everything else related to the Maple Leaf Gardens and business operations. That's when things started to go badly. While the Leafs failed to make it four Stanley Cups in a row in 1965, the Maple Leaf

Gardens company was raking in record profits. Ballard brought the Beatles to the Gardens that year, and to maximize his profits on that hot day in downtown Toronto, he delayed the show, turned up the heat, shut off the water fountains and sold only large cups of Coke to the 18,000 fans.

Conn Smythe could only watch from the sidelines as Ballard and his son began to change the way he had run his beloved franchise since 1927. The last straw for Conn Smythe came when Ballard announced that the Gardens would host a heavyweight boxing fight between Muhammad Ali and Ernie Terrell in the spring of 1966. Muhammad Ali had always been a controversial character, but he offended a lot of people in the United States and Canada because of his controversial comments about the Vietnam War. No city in the States or Canada would host the fight—until Ballard offered Maple Leaf Gardens. Conn Smythe was not happy about the decision. "A fight that isn't good enough for Chicago or Montréal certainly isn't good enough for Maple Leaf Gardens," said Smythe. He was so angered by the direction his beloved company was taking that he resigned his position as director, sold his remaining shares and left with a furious parting shot that would resonate among Maple Leafs faithful for decades: "I cannot go along with the policy of the present management to put cash ahead of class!"

On the ice, the Maple Leafs were struggling to find their identity. The Montréal Canadiens had returned to their old ways and eliminated the Leafs in the 1965 and 1966 playoffs on their way to two Stanley Cups. Montréal had a speedy, offensive-minded team under the watchful eye of head coach Toe Blake. The Canadiens and the Chicago Blackhawks were the two best teams during the 1966–67 season with their speedy, talent-laden clubs, while the Leafs battled their way through the regular season with a motley crew of young and old.

The 1966–67 season was the last for the "original six" teams before the league expanded to 12 teams in 1967–68. It was a decade of change, and in Canada's centennial year, two of the NHL's iconic teams would face off in one of the most memorable finals in history.

Since the Leafs' last Cup in 1964, Punch Imlach had surrounded himself with a group of over-the-hill veterans and a few wet-behind-the-ears rookies. Some of the veteran players should have been retired and playing on the golf course, but Imlach wanted players who had some experience in high-pressure situations and a desire to win above all else. They weren't just any old veterans, either. Imlach picked up legendary goaltender Terry Sawchuk, who had been in the league since 1950, from the Detroit Red Wings; the great Johnny Bower was still going strong at the age of 43; and there were all-stars Red Kelly, defenceman Allan Stanley and Marcel Pronovost all hovering around or over 40 years old.

Despite putting together the team he thought would dominate the regular season, Imlach's strategy was not without its many headaches. The Toronto coach had to check himself into hospital for stress and exhaustion when his Leafs went on a horrible 10-game losing streak. King Clancy replaced Imlach while he recovered, and the Leafs managed to turn things around, winning seven of their next 10 games and locking in third spot overall at the end of the regular season. It wasn't the greatest of finishes, but the team was healthy, Imlach was back where he belonged behind the bench, and they were feeling good about their chances against first-round opponents the Chicago Blackhawks.

The Blackhawks were offensive specialists with players like Bobby Hull, Stan Mikita, Kenny Wharram, and a young Phil Esposito all scoring a major part of the team's record 264 goals during the regular season. The Hawks also had the stellar goaltending of Vezina Trophy–winner Glenn Hall and Denis Dejordy, not making the Leafs' scoring task any easier. The Hawks were not lacking on defence, either, with Norris Trophy–winning defenceman Pierre Pilote and the imposing 6'3", 205-pound Doug Jarrett to stop any offensive threats the Leafs might throw at them. But the Hawks had a good team through most of the decade and only won the Stanley Cup once, in 1961. They just seemed to fall apart in the playoffs, and that's what Imlach was counting on this time.

With the power offence of the Blackhawks, Imlach knew he was going to have to rely on solid defence and some spectacular goaltending.

The Hawks came out fast in game one and proved many a sportswriter correct by winning easily by a score of 5–2. After that first game, however, it was all Toronto—or, more precisely, Terry Sawchuk. The Hawks managed to win one more game, but they could not get past Toronto's defence or their aggressive forechecking. The Leafs won the series in six games and the Hawks remained the proverbial underachievers they had been all decade. Searching for a reason for yet another elimination from the playoffs, Bobby Hull knew of only one: "I saw him [Sawchuk] make those saves, but I still can't believe it."

The Montréal Canadiens, meanwhile, had an easy time defeating the New York Rangers in four straight games, setting up the Stanley Cup final every Canadian had been hoping for: a classic battle of the two greatest rivals in hockey. It was Toronto versus Montréal.

Montréal was given the edge in the series by many observers, but the Canadiens only finished two points ahead of the Leafs during the regular season, so this was really anyone's Cup to win. The key for both teams was to get solid goaltending from their starters. The Leafs had won the last series against the Chicago Blackhawks on the strength of Terry Sawchuk's outstanding performance, and he would get the start for game one in Montréal. The Canadiens made a tough decision and decided to play rookie goaltender Rogie Vachon instead of the more experienced Gump Worsley and Charlie Hodge. Vachon had shown he was capable of stealing games during the regular season, playing in 19 games with a record of 11–3–4. Canadiens coach Toe Blake was counting on his young goaltender to be able to handle the pressure of Stanley Cup finals and give the Habs an advantage over the aged Leafs. Meanwhile, Vachon's inexperience was exactly what Punch Imlach was counting on, and before the fans even set foot in the building for the start of game one, the Toronto coach began his psychological campaign in the media.

After the Leafs' final practice before the first game, Imlach made sure to spare some time for the media so that the Canadiens would hear his message loud and clear: "Tell that cocky Junior B goaltender that he won't be facing New York Rangers peashooters when the Leafs open up on him. After we get through with Vachon, he may be back in Junior B," said Imlach, wearing a slight smirk.

The smirk would quickly disappear from Imlach's face when the Canadiens broke out for 6 goals on veteran Terry Sawchuk, while Vachon's play was excellent, allowing only 2 goals. The Canadiens were left wondering what had happened to the supposed competition the media had been hyping before the puck was even dropped. The problem for the Canadiens was that competition was coming in the next game, and its name was goaltender Johnny Bower.

In game two at the Montréal Forum, the Canadiens did everything they could to get a puck by Bower, but the wise goaltender was playing his angles perfectly that night and not letting out any juicy rebounds. The Leafs forwards, meanwhile, were doing what they were supposed to do, putting 3 goals behind young Vachon. When the final buzzer sounded, the scoreboard read Leafs 3, Canadiens 0. Bower was definitely the difference in the game, and he stole the show again in game three back in Toronto.

The Leafs played a decent game. Johnny Bower played the game of his life. Of the 54 shots the Canadiens managed to fire at him, he somehow stopped 52. The Leafs had some difficulty, but they managed to put 2 goals behind Vachon as well. All tied up, the two teams went into the first overtime period of the series. The first 20 minutes of overtime solved nothing. Both sides were too timid to open up the game, and that made for a limited number of shots on goal. Toronto decided to gamble and start the attack. Rogie Vachon stopped a couple of near chances, but the Leafs kept at it. Finally, Bob Pulford zipped a puck past Vachon for the winner. The Leafs were feeling confident after the overtime win, but their hopes deflated slightly when Johnny Bower pulled a muscle in the warm-up before game four. He wasn't going to be able to play for the rest of the series, so it was up to Terry Sawchuk to save the day. Unfortunately, Sawchuk was less than spectacular in his return to Stanley Cup play, giving up another 6 goals for a 6–2 final score. Sawchuk took all the blame for the loss, and the Canadiens were confident that they had his number. But

Sawchuk had been in such a place before during his time with the Red Wings in the '50s, and the goaltender called on that experience to put in his finest performance.

During game five, Sawchuk simply stood on his head to keep the Maple Leafs alive. Toronto's defence failed to present itself and left its veteran goaltender out to dry on many occasions, but the wily netminder was up to the task. On the Canadiens' end, Rogie Vachon was having an off night, and after the young player let in two soft goals, Toe Blake put veteran goaltender Gump Worsley to work for the remainder of the series in the hope that he could turn the Canadiens' fortunes around. The Habs did manage to sneak one goal by Sawchuk on a lucky deflection in front of the net, but they could get nothing else past him. The Leafs forwards helped Sawchuk's cause by putting two more goals by Worsley for a 4–1 final score. Toronto took a 3–2 series lead as the showdown headed back to Maple Leaf Gardens for the critical sixth game.

Head coach Toe Blake knew his Canadiens were in trouble. He had been around long enough to know when a team needed a few inspiring words, and before the start of game six, Blake stood in the centre of the dressing room and addressed his players. "Home ice won't be a factor until the seventh game. That's right—only in the seventh game, when we win the Cup!"

The Canadiens knew the key to their success was breaking Sawchuk. In the first few minutes of the game, they did everything possible to put the puck in the net, but the veteran goaltender was looking like his old self again, stopping everything that came his way. Maple Leaf Gardens erupted with joy when Red Kelly carried the puck into the Canadiens' zone and fired a shot at the net. Worsley made the leg save but let a big rebound out to a waiting Ron Ellis, who simply snapped the puck in the net for the go-ahead goal. The Leafs took the lead on a lucky break when an innocent passing play deflected off the leg of a Canadiens defenceman and into the net. Toronto's Jim Pappin was given credit for the goal because he had been the last on his team to touch the puck.

Third period. The Canadiens were going to have to pour on the desperation hockey if they wanted to prolong their stay in the Stanley Cup finals. Former Leafs player Dick Duff got some revenge on his old team when he deked the Toronto defence and put in a beautiful goal past Sawchuk. With the clock ticking late in the third period and the Leafs holding on to a slim margin,

Blake pulled Worsley in favour of an extra attacker. But the strategy backfired when Toronto's Red Kelly won the next faceoff in the Leafs zone and got the puck to Bob Pulford, who shot it down the length of the ice for the empty-net insurance goal. The Canadiens had simply run out of time. The final buzzer sounded and the Leafs players threw their gloves and sticks to the ice in celebration. The over-the-hill gang had defeated faster and younger teams against all the odds and took home one of the sweetest Cup victories in Maple Leafs history.

The city of Toronto savoured the victory over the Canadiens. The Leafs had defied the predictions and beat two of the best teams in the league to win the Stanley Cup. Few in the city realized, though, that this would be the last time they would get to call themselves Stanley Cup champions. It is now almost 40 years later, and still the city waits for another.

Chapter Ten

Times Are a-Changing

After winning the Cup in 1967, the Leafs began to change colour. They lost key players to retirement, trades and the expansion draft, and the ones who replaced them could not fill the void. Gone were key players Bob Baun, Red Kelly, Eddie Shack, Jim Pappin, Allan Stanley, Brian Conacher, Pete Stemkowski and Terry Sawchuk. Coming in was a set of skilled players including Paul Henderson, Pat Quinn, Norm Ullman and Jim Harrison, but they could not match the chemistry that existed in the Leafs organization prior to 1967. Behind the scenes, things were unraveling even quicker.

Ever since the early '60s, when Harold Ballard and Stafford Smythe took over operations of the Maple Leafs organization, they treated the company as a means to fund their personal needs. Beginning at that time, Ballard used the company to fund his own excesses, buying his son a motorcycle in 1965 and charging it to the Toronto farm team account, pretending the money was used to buy hockey sticks. He also charged the limousine service for his daughter's wedding to the Gardens, and when his home needed a new sprinkler system, it became $468 for the Gardens' sprinkler system. The suspicious accounting practices continued to pile up, growing more expensive and elaborate with each charge. A company that was renovating the Gardens was also hired to do renovations on Stafford's and Ballard's homes at a cost of nearly $300,000. But when the Leafs treasurer got wind of all the misuse of Gardens money, the Royal Canadian Mounted Police were called in and charges were filed against the two men.

With the charges weighing heavily on his mind, Stafford Smythe slowly began to descend into depression. He began to drink, and before his trial was scheduled to start in October 1971, he was admitted to hospital. A bleeding ulcer was causing him to throw up blood, and an emergency operation was needed to remove most of his stomach. A few days later, Smythe gave in to the ailment and died on October 13, 1971.

While charges still loomed over Ballard's head, he made a sneaky move to wrestle Stafford Smythe's shares in the Gardens away from the

Smythe family. Now with 70-percent control, he was the undisputed leader of the Toronto Maple Leafs. Not even Conn Smythe had enjoyed that much control over his beloved team.

The income taxes that the Gardens owed the federal government were quickly paid off after Ballard assumed control, but the fraud charges were still awaiting a verdict from the courts. In the highly publicized trial, Ballard had the best lawyers on his side, but he still could not get past the mountain of evidence against him.

"It wasn't a tough case," said prosecutor Clay Powell, who worked on the case. "We had the documents. We had the witnesses. I knew we had Smythe and Ballard cold."

The verdict was written in stone before the trial even ended. "You were in a position of trust," said Judge Harry Deyman upon sentencing Ballard, "and you violated that trust." The majority owner of the Toronto Maple Leafs was sentenced to jail for three years starting October 20, 1972. With time off for good behaviour, Ballard was back in control of the team just one year later, ready to devote all his energy to the destruction of the Toronto Maple Leafs.

The only good news to come out of Toronto in 1972 was that Leafs forward Paul Henderson scored the game-winning goal in 1972 Summit Series that had Canada battling the Soviet Union for the title of best hockey nation in the world. With a few swipes of his stick, Paul Henderson proved just that, and for his efforts, he remains one of the best-remembered Leafs of his time.

Meanwhile on the ice, the Maple Leafs were struggling with disappointing seasons and early playoff losses. After missing the playoffs in 1968 and an early exit from the 1969 playoffs at the hands of the talented Boston Bruins, coach and general manager Punch Imlach was promptly fired. When Ballard assumed control of hockey operations after Stafford Smythe's death, he never could make up his mind when it came to hiring a head coach or general manager. From 1972 to 1990, he hired and fired nine coaches: John McLellan, Red Kelly, Roger Neilson, Floyd Smith, Joe Crozier, Mike Nykoluk, Dan Maloney, John Brophy and George Armstrong. General managers had a difficult time keeping their jobs, as well. Punch Imlach (twice), Jim Gregory, Gerry McNamara and Gord Stellick all received their walking papers while Ballard was in charge.

While the Boston Bruins, Philadelphia Flyers and Montréal Canadiens dominated the '70s, the Maple Leafs struggled through the seasons and made several early exits from the playoffs. But it was not all doom and gloom for Leafs fans. A few players stepped above the antics of the people behind the scenes and kept the fans coming to the Gardens.

For the 1970–71 season, Jacques Plante joined the Maple Leafs organization and led the league with the lowest goals-against average of 1.88. Young Darryl Sittler began making a name for himself as the Leafs' top scorer in the '70s, with his most memorable year coming during the 1975–76 season.

On February 6, 1976, Sittler had the game of his life when he scored 6 goals and assisted on 4 others as the Toronto Maple Leafs beat up on the Boston Bruins 11–4. In nets for the Bruins was a poor young rookie goaltender named Dave Reece, who received the unfortunate nickname of "In-the-wrong-place-at-the-wrong-time Reece."

Sittler would have another outstanding performance in one game during the quarterfinals of the 1976 playoffs against the Philadelphia Flyers. He tied Rocket Richard's mark of 5 goals in a playoff game as the Leafs defeated the Flyers 8–5. Unfortunately, the Leafs lost the series.

Another player quickly found his way into the hearts of Toronto fans for his scoring ability and colourful personality. Lanny McDonald had his best years with the Leafs in the late '70s, scoring 47 goals in the 1977–78 regular season. But perhaps his greatest moment came in the 1978 playoffs against the New York Islanders. After a hard-fought series that twice went into overtime, the Leafs managed to force a deciding game seven. The Leafs pressed while goaltender Mike Palmateer kept Toronto in the game. When the third period buzzer sounded, the game was tied and headed into overtime. The Leafs got their first real break at 4:13 of the overtime period when the puck found its way onto Lanny McDonald's stick and he found himself alone on a break against Islanders goaltender Chico Resch. McDonald would not have been the coach's first choice for an overtime breakaway opportunity after suffering a broken bone in his wrist, a cut over his eye and a broken nose, but the mustachioed forward made his way in on Resch and put in the series winner past the Islanders goaltender. It was the first time Toronto had advanced past the quarterfinal round since the 1967 Cup win. Unfortunately for the Leafs, they would meet up with their old rivals, the Montréal Canadiens, who easily eliminated Toronto in four straight games.

Despite the Leafs' success in the late '70s, Ballard managed to mess things up. Coaches came and went, so did players, and by the 1979–80 season the Leafs were back near the bottom of their division. They barely made it into the playoffs only to lose against the Minnesota North Stars in the preliminary round in three straight games.

The 1980s is the decade every Leafs fan would like to gloss over when looking at the team's history. There were some moments and players to be proud of, but every year in the decade brought another losing record and early exits from the playoffs—when the Leafs were lucky enough to get in. There were standout players such as Wilf Paiement (40 goals and 57 assists in 1980–81), Rick Vaive (52 goals and 41 assists in 1983–84) and Gary Leeman (51 goals and 44 assists in 1989–90), but the disappointments were becoming too much to bear. The Leafs had become a joke to many professional eyes because of bad play and even worse management. It got so bad that even former Leafs coach Roger Neilson said of his former team, "Playing the Leafs is like eating Chinese food. Ten minutes later you want to play them again."

The Maple Leafs also lost the man who had been a member of the Toronto family since 1930. King Clancy, who had been a player, coach and Leafs ambassador during his time with the club, was kept around in his later years to cheer up

Ballard and regale anyone who would listen with stories from the Leafs' golden years. But after a gall bladder operation at the age of 86, Clancy passed away in late November 1986.

Fortunes had to change in Toronto, and it took the death of another member of the franchise's family to bring about the changes necessary to bring some respect back to the Leafs.

Chapter Eleven

The Return to Respectability

Suffering from diabetes for most of his life, Harold Ballard had always refused to listen to doctors' orders. He regularly gorged on chocolate, resulting in several blackouts, and he was generally in poor health during the 1980s. At one point, he required prostate surgery and a quintuple bypass to stop him from certain death. The power-mad Ballard had shunned everyone out of his life, and near the end only a few seemed to care as his health deteriorated. By February 1990, he was declared unfit to run the Maple Leafs operations; just a few months later, on April 11, 1990, the man who had taken the Leafs from the top of the league straight to the bottom ranks passed away at the age of 86 from kidney and heart failure.

Ballard had taken the great empire that was the Toronto Maple Leafs and reduced the team to the laughingstock of the National Hockey

League. The franchise was in need of a complete overhaul. When Ballard first attached himself to the Leafs organization, it had six minor-league affiliates from which to pick the best players. When Ballard passed away, the Leafs only had one. There was no overnight fix to the problem. It would take a few years before the Leafs would see the light at the end of the dark tunnel Ballard had built around the team.

Three men were assigned the Herculean task of rebuilding the shattered franchise: Donald Giffin, Steve Stavro and Donald Crump. Their first task—after paying off the massive debts incurred by Ballard—was to restore the reputation of the franchise and the on-ice success of the team. They replaced the old Stanley Cup banners that Ballard had removed, Conn Smythe's old office was reopened after years of use as a storage locker, and new facilities were added for the players.

On the hockey side of things, Giffin hired Floyd Smith to oversee operations. Smith saw that the Leafs could score but needed a solid defensive base, some larger players up front, and most importantly, a franchise goaltender. The Leafs goalies for the 1989–90 season were recording high averages that were not the mark of successful teams: Alan Bester had a 4.49, Peter Ing a 5.93 and Jeff Reese a 4.41.

The 1990 NHL draft held in Vancouver was the start of a new era for the Leafs. Toronto's first pick was a beefy young defenceman named Drake Berehowsky, but it would be the second pick that would bring the Leafs out of the hole and back into contention. Smith needed a goalie, but the Calgary Flames had already selected the top goaltender, Trevor Kidd. The next goalie in line was a kid named Felix Potvin. He had been a backup for Kidd during the World Junior Championships and was thought to have the potential to become a number one netminder. Smith selected Potvin 31st overall. The other goaltenders were left to fight for a spot while Potvin trained with the farm team, waiting for his opportunity to enter the big leagues.

Meanwhile, the Leafs continued searching for that elusive ingredient that would bring them success on the ice. The 1990–91 season saw the Leafs finish last in the division with a record of 23–46–11. There was a slight improvement for 1991–92 with a record of 30–43–7, but the Leafs were still last in their division.

The Leafs had made their biggest change off the ice in the summer of 1991 when Floyd Smith was removed from hockey operations and the job of general manager was given to Cliff Fletcher, a former Calgary Flames general manager. Fletcher set out immediately with some changes that would bring the Leafs the closest they had been to the Cup since they won in 1967 and return respectability to one of the greatest teams in hockey history.

"This is the greatest franchise in the National Hockey League...I want to reconfirm the pride and tradition of this great hockey club," Fletcher said at his first news conference as the Leafs' new general manager.

Fletcher knew that a team had to be built from the goaltender out, and he immediately traded Vincent Damphousse, Luke Richardson, goalie Peter Ing and Scott Thornton for Grant Fuhr, Glenn Anderson, Craig Berube and future considerations, which he used to get Ken Linseman. The Leafs now had a veteran goaltender in Fuhr, who could win them a few games on his own, and a few big names with Glenn Anderson and Berube, which would please the fans. But after a disappointing season in 1991–92, Fletcher knew he needed to make a major change, and near the end of the regular season, he got wind of an unhappy player in Calgary who just might change the Leafs' fortunes.

Doug Gilmour had been an integral part of the Calgary Flames' success since he helped them to the Stanley Cup in 1989, but he had grown tired of the management and was demanding more money. Fletcher got word of Gilmour's unhappiness and immediately called Flames GM Doug Risebrough. After talking through the trade possibilities, Risebrough and Fletcher came to an agreement. The trade would be one of the most important in Leafs history and turned the franchise's fortunes completely around. In the middle of the season, the Calgary Flames traded Doug Gilmour, Jamie Macoun, Ric Nattress, Kent Manderville and Rick Wamsley in return for Gary Leeman, Michel Petit, Alexander Godynyuk, Craig Berube and Jeff Reese. The Leafs wanted Gilmour most because he was touted as the franchise player they needed. Gilmour was an excellent two-way player, able to make passes and score beautifully while being just as effective on defence.

Felix Potvin got his feet wet in a few games during the 1991–92 regular season and would be called up from the minors the next season to help the Leafs to their best showing in over a decade. Another new face was set to make his debut behind the bench after spending several successful years with the Montréal Canadiens. Pat Burns was a tough, no-nonsense kind of coach, and his style seemed to work well with the team of veterans and rookies manager Cliff Fletcher had cobbled together.

Halfway through the 1992–93 season, Fletcher was looking like a genius as the Leafs had seemingly turned their franchise around in just one season. People even began to talk about possible post-season success. Doug Gilmour was winning new fans with each game and had his biggest fan in sportscaster and former NHL coach Don Cherry. Cherry often extolled Gilmour's skill and ability on his popular Saturday night hockey show, *Coach's Corner*, and after one game Cherry literally showed his love for the forward when he described him as the "best hockey player in the world" and then kissed the Leafs forward on camera.

With all parts of the organization in order, the Leafs finished off the season with a record of 44–29–11. Doug Gilmour was the Leafs' top scorer with 32 goals and 95 assists for 127 points. Felix Potvin also impressed many people and found himself a regular spot in the lineup, finishing the season with a goals-against average of 2.50. But it was in the playoffs where the Leafs really stepped up their game and brought some life back to Maple Leaf Gardens.

Things didn't start out so well for the Leafs in the opening round against the Detroit Red Wings. They lost the first two games by scores of 6–3 and 6–2 and looked completely outplayed in every aspect. Criticism for the losses fell immediately on the head of captain Wendel Clark for his alleged disinterest in the two games. Clark responded to the criticism from the media by scoring the game-winning goal in a 4–2 victory in game three.

"If people judge your play, that's part of living in Toronto. You start taking that stuff personally, you go in the mental home," Wendel Clark said after the game.

Another Leafs player began to step up to the pressure and take control of the series. A late-season addition, Dave Andreychuk had not produced the results he was capable of during the regular season or the first two games of the post-season. But in game three he scored 2 goals, and in game four, fans were once again cheering him when he scored two more to help the Leafs to a close 3–2 victory. In game five, Toronto took the lead in the series for the first time with an exciting 5–4 overtime victory. The Leafs closely checked Detroit captain Steve Yzerman all game, holding the sniper off the scoreboard. Mike Foligno put in the overtime winner.

The Red Wings went into the sixth game determined to extend the series. They had the firepower and they used it, scoring 7 goals on an average-looking Potvin while the Leafs could only score three. Game seven in Detroit belonged to one man, and his name was Doug Gilmour. Never once letting up his level of intensity, Gilmour worked in the corners, stood in front of the net, and did just about anything to ensure his team's success. Gilmour assisted on the Leafs' first goal by Glenn Anderson, and he did the grunt work on the second goal so that Bob Rouse could get open to score. In the third period, Gilmour took the game into his own hands with the Leafs trailing 3–2 and scored the tying goal, sending the game into overtime. With Felix Potvin holding down the fort for the Maple Leafs, the players knew if they just got one break they could end the series and move on to the next round. At 2:55 of the first overtime period, Gilmour wrestled the puck free from the corner and passed back to the point, where Rouse whipped in a shot that hit Leafs right-winger Nikolai Borschevsky's stick and bounced into the Detroit net. For the first time since the late '70s, Toronto Maple Leafs fans had reason to believe that their team could make an honest push for the Cup because the team had what it lacked for years: chemistry.

But nothing would be easy for the Leafs during the '93 playoffs. Up next were the St. Louis Blues, who had just defeated the skilled Chicago Blackhawks in four straight games mainly because of one person, goaltender Curtis Joseph. But Felix Potvin was also looking to do the same thing after a few embarrassing performances against Detroit. In the first two games of the series at Maple Leaf Gardens, the goaltenders were the stars.

Joseph put on a goaltending spectacle, stopping 62 shots in a game that went into double overtime. Potvin was getting better protection from his defensive line, but he still had to make his patented cat-like saves. Much to the delight of the thousands of Maple Leafs fans at the Gardens, Doug Gilmour scored the game-winner on Joseph at the three-minute mark of the second overtime period.

The same scenario played out in game two but this time, it was the Blues that came out on top after another stellar performance by Curtis Joseph. They took the momentum back with them to St. Louis and won the next game by another close margin of 4–3. Once again, Joseph stole the show. For games four and five, however, the Leafs turned their attention to Joseph and placed as many bodies in front of him as possible to get him off his game—and it worked. Joseph looked positively ordinary, and the Blues lost games four and five by scores of 4–1 and 5–1. The Blues managed to win game six by a close margin of 2–1, but the Leafs had the momentum in the series and they had finally figured out how to solve the Joseph problem. The Leafs put 6 goals past him while Felix Potvin did not let any pucks into his net. They won the game 6–0 and went into the Stanley Cup semifinals for the first time since 1978. Wayne Gretzky and the Los Angeles Kings were next.

It was another laborious series for the Leafs. They won the first game by a score of 4–1 but would trade the next few wins and fight several exciting overtime games, forcing another long series. Toronto came close to winning the whole thing, but Wayne Gretzky was the difference. In game six, he got away with murder when his stick clipped Doug Gilmour's face and opened up a cut that required eight stitches to repair. Referee Kerry Frasier did not see the infraction and play continued. The Kings' Luc Robitaille took control of the puck a few seconds later, spotted Gretzky on the open wing and hit him with the pass. Gretzky simply tapped it in for the winning goal in overtime. Los Angeles survived to force game seven. Gretzky had another stellar performance, leading the Kings to a narrow 5–4 victory.

The Leafs were upset over the way the series took a sudden turn, but they had played like true Stanley Cup winners and many fans had returned to the Gardens to see their team play like they used to.

The Leafs had another great regular season in 1993–94, finishing with 98 points. Doug Gilmour led the team again with 111 points while Dave Andreychuk scored a career-high 53 goals. In the playoffs, they handily made their way past the first round, defeating the Chicago Blackhawks in six games, then took the second round against the San Jose Sharks in an exciting seven-game series win and met up with the Vancouver Canucks in the conference finals. But the Canucks had the Leafs' number and took the series in just five games.

Two late exits in the playoffs left the Toronto Maple Leafs wondering what piece of the puzzle they were missing to complete the perfect team. For the lockout-shortened 1994–95 season, Fletcher thought the Leafs needed younger scoring talent and decided to go shopping in Québec City for a new player. Fletcher brokered a deal with Nordiques general manager Pierre Lacroix to trade fan favourite Wendel Clark, Sylvain Lefebvre, Landon Wilson and Rob Pearson for Mats Sundin, Garth Butcher, Todd Warriner and

Mike Ridley. But despite the addition of the new talent and a few decent seasons, the Leafs once again began to fail. They had several early exits from the playoffs and missed the post-season completely in 1997. Things seemed to be headed in the direction Leafs fans had gotten used to over the years. After the disappointment of 1997, Cliff Fletcher had decided his time with the Maple Leafs had come to an end, and he announced his resignation. Toronto owners immediately approached former goaltending great Ken Dryden to take over Fletcher's duties as president and general manager. But Dryden preferred to stay out of the limelight and eventually gave the general manager's position to Pat Quinn. With Dryden at the helm as president, the Leafs once again returned to a credible position in league standings.

There was an immediate turnaround for the 1998–99 season for three main reasons. First, the Leafs were taken out of the western conference and put back in to the east. Second, they signed all-star goaltender Curtis Joseph. Third, they hired general manager Pat Quinn to replace Mike Murphy as coach. They finished the season with the most goals in the NHL, and looked ready to make a push for the Cup after a few years out of serious contention. The Maple Leafs made their way past their first-round opponents the Philadelphia Flyers in six games and dispensed of a tough Pittsburgh Penguins squad in six as well, but they ran up against the Buffalo Sabers in the conference finals and lost in five games. It seemed as if the Leafs were cursed in the playoffs, having not seen a Stanley Cup final since 1967.

The year 1999 also saw the Maple Leafs move to a new home. Maple Leaf Gardens had been the team's home and one of hockey's greatest shrines since it opened on November 12, 1931. Under its lights, the fans of Toronto witnessed their favourite team win 11 Stanley Cups and play 2533 games with a record of 1125 wins, 786 losses and 346 ties. For hockey fans everywhere, when it was announced that the Leafs would be changing venues, it was hard to let go of that glorious past under the roof that Conn Smythe built. The building lost some of its mystique when Harold Ballard removed all the old memorabilia and the team fell into the longest slump in its history. Yet the old banners were replaced, the pictures were put back on the wall, and the Ballard years had been slowly wiped away, bringing the old feel of hockey's greatest temple back to the Gardens.

"If the Gardens could talk, what a story it would tell. The Gardens is more than just bricks, concrete and steel," said former Leafs player Brian Conacher. "It's the people through the years who made it the Mecca it became."

But the NHL was changing, and most teams were moving into bigger and more luxurious arenas. Even the famed Montréal Forum faded into memory when the Canadiens moved buildings in 1996. Construction began on the Maple Leafs' new arena on March 12, 1997. On February 20, 1999, the Leafs opened their new home, now dubbed the Air Canada Centre, with a loss to the Chicago Blackhawks, the same team they lost to when the Maple Leaf Gardens opened. The Air Canada Centre was a new, modern facility with roomy seats, luxurious boxes for corporate affairs, restaurants, bars and anything hockey fans might need, but the true home of the Leafs will always be within the walls of the Carlton Street Maple Leaf Gardens. "It was such an honest place to play hockey. I don't think they can build a building like this again," said Leafs old-timer Howie Meeker.

Over the next few years, the Leafs posted winning seasons but had terrible luck in the playoffs. In 2000 and 2001, they ran up against the defence and goaltending of the New Jersey Devils, who eliminated them on both occasions. In 2002, they made another run into the conference finals and met the Carolina Hurricanes. In a closely contested series, neither team scored more than 3 goals in a game, and three of the games went into overtime. Unfortunately for Toronto, the majority of the games were in favour of the Hurricanes.

The Leafs brought on veteran goaltender Ed Belfour for the 2002–03 season after several years with Curtis Joseph. Belfour brought a sense of competition and stability to the Leafs net that was desperately needed if they were going to make it anywhere in the post-season. But despite another winning regular season of 98 points, the Leafs were once again snake-bitten in the playoffs, losing to the Philadelphia Flyers in a tough seven-game series. Again, overtime games were their downfall. Three of the seven games went into double and triple overtime, but the Leafs could only manage to come out with one victory. In the end, it was that one victory they needed to get to the next round.

The next few seasons saw a few changes to the Maple Leafs lineup, but still, success in the playoffs eluded the team. Guys like Brian Leetch, Ron Francis, Owen Nolan and Joe Nieuwendyk helped on defence and with goal production, but that key ingredient was missing to propel them to greatness.

Most recently, the Toronto Maple Leafs fired long-time coach Pat Quinn at the end of the 2005–06 season after the team missed the playoffs for the first time since he joined the club in 1998. Five days after the end of the regulation season, Pat Quinn and assistant coach Rick Ley were relieved of their duties and replaced by Toronto Marlies and former Carolina Hurricanes head coach Paul Maurice.

With the loss of some veteran players, the Leafs bolstered their squad with the addition of goaltender Andrew Raycroft from the Boston Bruins, defencemen Hal Gill and Pavel Kubina, and gritty forward Michael Peca. With new coaching and a bunch of fresh faces, the Leafs started the 2006–07 NHL regular season on a positive note. But the test would be to keep the momentum alive during a season in which many predicted the team wouldn't even make the playoffs, and then they would need to make it to the Stanley Cup final.

The Stats

From 1917 to the present, the Toronto Maple Leafs have racked up some of the most amazing numbers in hockey history. Since the franchise first began operations in the National Hockey League in 1917 as the Toronto Arenas, it has won the Stanley Cup 13 times and established a tradition of winning that has seen the team through two name changes, several struggles for control of the franchise and the loss of some dear members of the Toronto family. Toronto has been able to achieve such great things in hockey because they have had some of the best players ever in the game. Red Kelly, Charlie Conacher, Darryl Sittler, Borje Salming and Mats Sundin are just a few of the loyal Toronto Maple Leafs who stuck with the team and made the biggest contribution to the franchise's history of success. Here are just a few of the most impressive Toronto Maple Leafs stats and facts.

Season and Playoff Record

Season	Team Name	GP	W	L	T	OTL	Pts	Playoffs
1917–18	Arenas	22	13	9	0	—	26	Won Stanley Cup
1918–19	Arenas	18	5	13	0	—	10	Out of playoffs
1919–20	St. Patricks	24	12	12	0	—	24	Out of playoffs
1920–21	St. Patricks	24	15	9	0	—	30	Lost final
1921–22	St. Patricks	24	13	10	1	—	27	Won Stanley Cup
1922–23	St. Patricks	24	13	10	1	—	27	Out of playoffs
1923–24	St. Patricks	24	10	14	0	—	20	Out of playoffs
1924–25	St. Patricks	30	19	11	0	—	38	Lost semifinal
1925–26	St. Patricks	36	12	21	3	—	27	Out of playoffs
1926–27	St. Pats/Leafs	44	15	24	5	—	35	Out of playoffs
1927–28	Maple Leafs	44	18	18	8	—	44	Out of playoffs
1928–29	Maple Leafs	44	21	18	5	—	47	Lost in 2nd round
1929–30	Maple Leafs	44	17	21	6	—	40	Out of playoffs
1930–31	Maple Leafs	44	22	13	9	—	53	Lost in 1st round
1931–32	Maple Leafs	48	23	18	7	—	53	Won Stanley Cup
1932–33	Maple Leafs	48	24	18	6	—	54	Lost final
1933–34	Maple Leafs	48	26	13	9	—	61	Lost semifinal
1934–35	Maple Leafs	48	30	14	4	—	64	Lost final
1935–36	Maple Leafs	48	23	19	6	—	52	Lost final
1936–37	Maple Leafs	48	22	21	5	—	49	Lost quarterfinals
1937–38	Maple Leafs	48	24	15	9	—	57	Lost final
1938–39	Maple Leafs	48	19	20	9	—	47	Lost final
1939–40	Maple Leafs	48	25	17	6	—	56	Lost final
1940–41	Maple Leafs	48	28	14	6	—	62	Lost semifinal
1941–42	Maple Leafs	48	27	18	3	—	57	Won Stanley Cup
1942–43	Maple Leafs	50	22	19	9	—	53	Lost final
1943–44	Maple Leafs	50	23	23	4	—	50	Lost semifinal
1944–45	Maple Leafs	50	24	22	4	—	52	Won Stanley Cup
1945–46	Maple Leafs	50	19	24	7	—	45	Out of playoffs
1946–47	Maple Leafs	60	31	19	10	—	72	Won Stanley Cup
1947–48	Maple Leafs	60	32	15	13	—	77	Won Stanley Cup

Season and Playoff Record continued

Season	Team Name	GP	W	L	T	OTL	Pts	Playoffs
1948–49	Maple Leafs	60	22	25	13	—	57	Won Stanley Cup
1949–50	Maple Leafs	70	31	27	12	—	74	Lost in 1st round
1950–51	Maple Leafs	70	41	16	13	—	95	Won Stanley Cup
1951–52	Maple Leafs	70	29	25	16	—	74	Lost semifinal
1952–53	Maple Leafs	70	27	30	13	—	67	Out of playoffs
1953–54	Maple Leafs	70	32	24	14	—	78	Lost semifinal
1954–55	Maple Leafs	70	24	24	22	—	70	Lost semifinal
1955–56	Maple Leafs	70	24	33	13	—	61	Out of playoffs
1956–57	Maple Leafs	70	21	34	15	—	57	Out of playoffs
1957–58	Maple Leafs	70	21	38	11	—	53	Out of playoffs
1958–59	Maple Leafs	70	27	32	11	—	65	Lost final
1959–60	Maple Leafs	70	35	26	9	—	79	Lost final
1960–61	Maple Leafs	70	39	19	12	—	90	Lost semifinal
1961–62	Maple Leafs	70	37	22	11	—	85	Won Stanley Cup
1962–63	Maple Leafs	70	35	23	12	—	82	Won Stanley Cup
1963–64	Maple Leafs	70	33	25	12	—	78	Won Stanley Cup
1964–65	Maple Leafs	70	30	26	14	—	74	Lost semifinal
1965–66	Maple Leafs	70	34	25	11	—	79	Lost semifinal
1966–67	Maple Leafs	70	32	27	11	—	75	Won Stanley Cup
1967–68	Maple Leafs	74	33	31	10	—	76	Out of playoffs
1968–69	Maple Leafs	76	35	26	15	—	85	Lost quarterfinal
1969–70	Maple Leafs	76	29	34	13	—	71	Out of playoffs
1970–71	Maple Leafs	78	37	33	8	—	82	Lost quarterfinal
1971–72	Maple Leafs	78	33	31	14	—	80	Lost quarterfinal
1972–73	Maple Leafs	78	27	41	10	—	64	Out of playoffs
1973–74	Maple Leafs	78	35	27	16	—	86	Lost quarterfinal
1974–75	Maple Leafs	80	31	33	16	—	78	Lost quarterfinal
1975–76	Maple Leafs	80	34	31	15	—	83	Lost quarterfinal
1976–77	Maple Leafs	80	33	32	15	—	81	Lost quarterfinal
1977–78	Maple Leafs	80	41	29	10	—	92	Lost semifinal
1978–79	Maple Leafs	80	34	33	13	—	81	Lost quarterfinal
1979–80	Maple Leafs	80	35	40	5	—	75	Lost prelim. round
1980–81	Maple Leafs	80	28	37	15	—	71	Lost prelim. round
1981–82	Maple Leafs	80	20	44	16	—	56	Out of playoffs

Season and Playoff Record continued

Season	Team Name	GP	W	L	T	OTL	Pts	Playoffs
1982–83	Maple Leafs	80	28	40	12	—	68	Lost 1st round
1983–84	Maple Leafs	80	26	45	9	—	61	Out of playoffs
1984–85	Maple Leafs	80	20	52	8	—	48	Out of playoffs
1985–86	Maple Leafs	80	25	48	7	—	57	Lost Norris final
1986–87	Maple Leafs	80	32	42	6	—	70	Lost Norris final
1987–88	Maple Leafs	80	21	49	10	—	52	Lost in 1st round
1988–89	Maple Leafs	80	28	46	6	—	62	Out of playoffs
1989–90	Maple Leafs	80	38	38	4	—	80	Lost preliminary
1990–91	Maple Leafs	80	23	46	11	—	57	Out of playoffs
1991–92	Maple Leafs	80	30	43	7	—	67	Out of playoffs
1992–93	Maple Leafs	84	44	29	11	—	99	Lost Conference final
1993–94	Maple Leafs	84	43	29	12	—	98	Lost Conference final
1994–95	Maple Leafs	48	21	19	8	—	50	Lost in 1st round
1995–96	Maple Leafs	82	34	36	12	—	80	Lost in 1st round
1996–97	Maple Leafs	82	30	44	8	—	68	Out of playoffs
1997–98	Maple Leafs	82	30	43	9	—	69	Out of playoffs
1998–99	Maple Leafs	82	45	30	7	—	97	Lost Conference final
1999–00	Maple Leafs	82	45	27	7	3	100	Lost in 2nd round
2000–01	Maple Leafs	82	37	29	11	5	90	Lost in 2nd round
2001–02	Maple Leafs	82	43	25	10	4	100	Lost Conference final
2002–03	Maple Leafs	82	44	28	7	3	98	Lost in 1st round
2003–04	Maple Leafs	82	45	24	10	3	103	Lost in 2nd round
2004–05	Maple Leafs	—	—	—	—	—	—	Lockout
2005–06	Maple Leafs	82	41	33	—	8	90	Out of Playoffs
2006–07	Maple Leafs				—			Season Ongoing
Grand Total	Maple Leafs	5612	2448	2353	783	25	5711	—

Individual Career Records

Most Seasons

21, George Armstrong

20, Tim Horton

16, Ron Ellis

Most Games Played

1187, George Armstrong

1185, Tim Horton

1099, Borje Salming

Longest Consecutive Game Streak

486, Tim Horton, February 11, 1961,
to February 4, 1968

Most Goals

389, Darryl Sittler

365, Dave Keon

361, Mats Sundin

Most Goals by a Defenceman

148, Borje Salming

112, Ian Turnbull

109, Tim Horton

Most Assists

620, Borje Salming

527, Darryl Sittler

493, Dave Keon

Most Points

916, Darryl Sittler

858, Dave Keon

833, Mats Sundin

Most Penalty Minutes

2265, Tie Domi

1670, Dave "Tiger" Williams

1535, Wendel Clark

Individual Single-Game Records

Most Goals

6, Darryl Sittler: February 7, 1976, versus Boston Bruins

Most Goals by a Defenceman

5, Ian Turnbull: February 2, 1977, versus Detroit Red Wings

Most Goals in One Period

4, Harvey "Busher" Jackson: November 20, 1934, versus St. Louis Eagles

Fastest Goal, Start of Game

0:07, Charlie Conacher: February 6, 1932, versus Boston Bruins

0:08, Ted Kennedy: October 24, 1953, versus Boston Bruins

Most Assists

6, Doug Gilmour: February 13, 1993, versus Minnesota North Stars

Most Assists by a Defenceman

6, Walter "Babe" Pratt: January 8, 1944, versus Boston Bruins

Most Points in One Game

10, Darryl Sittler: February 7, 1976, versus Boston Bruins

Most Points by a Defenceman

6, Walter "Babe" Pratt: January 8, 1944, versus Boston Bruins

Most Penalty Minutes

57, Brad Smith: November 15, 1986

Most Penalties

9, Jim Dorey: October 16, 1968

Hall of Fame Builders

Harold E. Ballard

Cliff Fletcher

Foster Hewitt

Punch Imlach

Roger Neilson

Conn Smythe

Frank J. Selke

Numbers Retired by the Maple Leafs

#5, Bill Barilko

#6, Ace Bailey

Honoured Numbers

#1, Turk Broda and Johnny Bower

#4, Hap Day and Red Kelly

#7, King Clancy and Tim Horton

#9, Charlie Conacher and Ted Kennedy

#10, Syl Apps and George Armstrong

#21, Borje Salming

#27, Frank Mahovlich and Darryl Sittler

Notes on Sources

Batten, Jack. *The Leafs: An Anecdotal History of the Toronto Maple Leafs*. Toronto: Key Porter Books, 1994.

Cox, Damien, and Gord Stellick. *'67: The Maple Leafs, Their Sensational Victory, and the End of an Empire*. Toronto: Wiley, 2004.

Diamond, Dan, ed. *Total NHL*. Toronto: Dan Diamond and Associates, 2003.

Diamond, Dan, and Eric Zweig. *Hockey's Glory Days: The 1950s and '60s*. Kansas City: Andrews McMeel Publishing, 2003.

Hornby, Lance. *Hockey's Greatest Moment*. Toronto: Key Porter Books, 2004.

Leonetti, Mike. *Maple Leaf Legends*. Vancouver: Raincoast Books, 2002.

McDonnell, Chris. *Hockey's Greatest Stars: Legends and Young Lions*. Willowdale: Firefly Books, 1999.

McFarlane, Brian. *Best of the Orginal Six*. Bolton: Fenn Publishing, 2004.

Podnieks, Andrew, et al. *Kings of the Ice: A History of World Hockey*. Richmond Hill: NDE Publishing, 2002.

Podnieks, Andrew. *Return to Glory.* Toronto: ECW Press, 1995.

Turowetz, Allan, and Goyens, Chrys. *Lions In Winter.* Scarborough: Prentice Hall, 1986.

J. Alexander Poulton

J. Alexander Poulton is a writer and photographer and has been a genuine enthusiast of Canada's national pastime ever since seeing his first hockey game. His favourite memory was meeting the legendary gentleman hockey player Jean Béliveau, who in 1988 towered over the young awe-struck author.

He earned his B.A. in English Literature from McGill University and his graduate diploma in Journalism from Concordia University. He has five other books to his credit: *Canadian Hockey Record Breakers, Greatest Moments in Canadian Hockey, Greatest Games of the Stanley Cup, The Montréal Canadiens* and *Greatest Goalies of the NHL.*

OverTime Books

If you enjoyed *The Toronto Maple Leafs*, be sure to check out these other great titles from OverTime Books:

THE MONTRÉAL CANADIENS: The History & Players behind Hockey's Most Legendary Team
by J. Alexander Poulton
The Montréal Canadiens are the oldest established NHL franchise and the second most successful professional sports club in North American sports history. J. Alexander Poulton, whose father worked for the Canadiens, provides this look back at a legendary team from which a great many superstars emerged.
Softcover • 5.25" X 8.25" • 168 pages • ISBN10 1-897277-09-1 • ISBN13 978-1897277-09-6
• $9.95

THE EDMONTON OILERS: The Players, Games & Stories behind Hockey's Legendary Team
by Peter Boer
Take a look at the winningest expansion team in the history of the NHL. Since 1972, the Edmonton Oilers have been on a roller coaster, enjoying one Stanley Cup victory after another followed by many seasons out of the playoffs. Here is the story of the team that helped make Edmonton the City of Champions.
Softcover • 5.25" X 8.25" • 168 pages • ISBN10 1-897277-02-4 • ISBN13 978-1897277-02-7
• $9.95

NHL ENFORCERS: The Rough and Tough Guys of Hockey
by Arpon Basu
Throughout the history of professional hockey, the tough guys of the game have done much to define hockey, both for better and for worse. Read about enforcers such as Eddie Shore, Tie Domi, "Tiger" Williams, Bob Probert and so many more.
Softcover • 5.25" X 8.25" • 168 pages • ISBN10 1-897277-10-5 • ISBN13 978-1897277-10-2
• $9.95

GREATEST STANLEY CUP VICTORIES: The Battles and the Rivalries
by J. Alexander Poulton
A look back at some of the NHL's most memorable battles for hockey supremacy.
Softcover • 5.25" X 8.25" • 168 pages • ISBN10 1-897277-06-7 • ISBN13 978-1897277-06-5
• $9.95

HOCKEY'S HOTTEST PLAYERS: The On- & Off-Ice Stories of the Superstars
by Arpon Basu
Sports journalist Arpon Basu profiles today's rising stars in the National Hockey League. He looks not only at their on-ice performance and statistics but also probes the human story behind their victories and struggles, revealing the journey they've taken to reach the highest echelons of their sport.
Softcover • 5.25" X 8.25" • 144 pages • ISBN10 0-9737681-3-4 • ISBN13 978-0-9737681-3-8
• $9.95

CANADIAN HOCKEY TRIVIA: The Facts, Stats & Strange Tales of Canadian Hockey
by J. Alexander Poulton
Hockey is so much a part of Canadian life that the theme song to Hockey Night in Canada has been called our unofficial national anthem. Read the fascinating facts from Canada's favorite game such as the almost-forgotten Winnipeg Falcons, who were the first Canadian team to win Olympic gold in 1920 and Dennis O'Brien, who holds the record for most NHL teams played for in a single season.
Softcover • 5.25" X 8.25" • 168 pages • ISBN10 1-897277-01-6 • ISBN13 978-1-897277-01-0
• $9.95

Lone Pine Publishing is the exclusive distributor for OverTime Books.
If you cannot find these titles at your local bookstore, contact us:

Canada: 1-800-661-9017   USA: 1-800-518-3541